STRONGER THAN PRISON WALLS

By the same author

TORTURED FOR CHRIST
UNDERGROUND SAINTS

STRONGER THAN PRISON WALLS

RICHARD WURMBRAND

Direct from years of solitary confinement in a Communist
prison come these messages of faith and courage

Fleming H. Revell Company
Old Tappan, New Jersey

Stronger Than Prison Walls, published by the Fleming H. Revell Company, is the United States edition of *Sermons in Solitary Confinement,* first published in 1969 by Hodder and Stoughton Limited in the United Kingdom.

SBN 8007-0412-6

Copyright © 1969 by Richard Wurmbrand,
Published by the Fleming H. Revell Company,
Old Tappan, New Jersey
Library of Congress Catalog Card Number: 78-123056
Printed in the United States of America

Contents

Preface

Out of fourteen years in jail under the Communists in Rumania, I spent three years alone in a cell thirty feet below ground, never seeing sun, moon or stars, flowers or snow, never seeing another man except for the guards and interrogators who beat and tortured me.

I seldom heard a noise in that prison. The guards had felt-soled shoes and I did not hear their approach.

I had no Bible, nor any other book. I had no paper on which to write my thoughts. The only things we were expected to write were statements accusing ourselves and others.

During that time I rarely slept at night. I slept in the daytime. Every night I passed the hours in spiritual exercises and prayer. Every night I composed a sermon and delivered it.

I had a faint hope that one day I might be released. And so I tried to memorise the sermons. In order to do this, I used a device of putting the main ideas into short rhymes. There are precedents for this. Omar Kayyam, Nostradamus, Heinrich Seuse and Angelus Silesius all condensed into extremely short verses a wealth of philosophy, religion and prophecy. So I composed my rhymes. These I learned by heart and kept in my memory through continual repetition. When my mind broke down under the influence of heavy doping, I forgot them. But as the effects of the drugs passed, they came vividly back to me.

Here are just a few of the sermons. My unusually good memory retains some three hundred and fifty.

These sermons are not to be judged for their dogmatic content. I did not live on dogma then. Nobody can. The soul feeds on Christ, not on teachings about him.

From the dogmatic point of view, David and Job were wrong

to argue with God. From the dogmatic point of view, the author of the book of Esther was wrong not to write one word of praise for the God who had just wrought such a great deliverance for his people. From the dogmatic point of view, St. John the Baptist was wrong when in prison he questioned the fact that Jesus was the Messiah. Dogmatists could even find fault with Jesus himself. He ought not to have trembled in Gethsemane. But life, even religious life, is not concerned with dogmas. It pursues its own course, and that course seems foolish to reason.

I have lived in exceptional circumstances and passed through exceptional states of spirit. I must share these with my fellowmen. They need to be known, because even now tens of thousands of Christians are in prison in Communist countries, tortured and drugged and kept in solitary cells and put in strait-jackets as I have been. Many of them must have similar reactions to mine. Jesus, in his compassion for the multitudes, became one of them, a carpenter in a poor country among an oppressed people. You cannot have compassion (the word means suffering together) unless you know the state of heart of those who are suffering.

To be in a solitary cell under the Communists or the Nazis is to reach the peak of suffering. The reactions of Christians who pass through such trials are something apart from everything else.

The purpose of this book is to make these thoughts and feelings known to those who are on the side of the innocent victims. With many of the thoughts expressed in these sermons I no longer agree myself any more, now that I am living under normal conditions. But I record my thoughts as they occurred to me then.

Reader, instead of judging, enter into fellowship with your Christian brothers who are in prison in situations where, to use the words of Bede, "there is no voice but of weeping, no face but of the tormentors". Put yourself in their situation; "remember them that are in bonds as bound with them".[1] Use your imagination to feel what it is like to be in solitary confinement and tortured. Only then will you be able to understand this book.

It contains the sermons of a pastor whose pillars of reason rocked under strain, as I recognise now. There were times when I was near to apostasy. Happily, just on those worst days I was not tortured. Probably I would have cracked then. The tortures happened only after I had overcome despair.

It has been easy for me to reconstruct the whole sermon out of a short poem, because while I left the solitary cell the solitary cell has never left me. Not one day passes without my living in it, whether I am in a large rally in the United States, in a church or a committee meeting in Britain, or just sitting in a train. My real being has remained for ever in solitary confinement. I don't so much live my present life, as relive continually those prison years. This is not because they are an essential part of my personal history but because I am not the real me. The real me is those who are in lonely, dreary, damp cells today, in Red China, in Albania, in Rumania, in North Korea and other Communist countries. They are the little brothers of Jesus. They are the most precious part of the mystical body of Christ on earth. I am living their life when I relive my years of solitary confinement. It is a strange experience. It may lead to madness. There may already be madness in these sermons of mine.

But if Erasmus was right when he wrote *In Praise of Folly*, why should not folly be allowed to speak for itself? Communism has driven mad many pastors and other Christians, whose mental health broke down under prolonged torture. Why should only wise men say what they think about Communism? Why not let the mad speak out of their madness? It is the maddened thoughts of those who are kept in conditions of hardship beyond description that I here put down on paper.

I have had moments of knowing the victory of faith in prison. I have also had moments of despair. I thank God for both. The latter had some good in them, in that they showed me my limitations and taught me not to rely on my own victories, nor on my faith, but on the atoning blood of Jesus Christ.

New causes always produce new effects. Solitary confinement under the Communists is something new in church history. It cannot be compared with the Roman or even the Nazi persecutions. Consider the difference made by the fact of intensive doping or scientific brainwashing, and don't be surprised at our thoughts and reactions.

I am conscious that some of the speculations in these sermons are bold, with a boldness that can come only from a long term of silence. Do they represent the truth, or are they heresy? Truth is the correspondence between thought and reality. But does anyone know the whole reality? We lived in a reality apart, and our thoughts may have mirrored it correctly, although it seems strange to those who live a quiet, normal life. In any case, that is how I thought then. The minds of thousands of Christians who are tortured in Communist prisons today are battered by just such tempests. This is what I have to put on paper, for the benefit of those Christians who do not wish to lead selfish lives but to have fellowship with those who are passing through not only physical tortures but also extreme spiritual tension.

And now let me tell you the words of the psalmist: "Hearken, O daughter, and consider, and incline thine ear. Forget also thine own people (whether you are Catholic or Protestant, fundamentalist or radical), and thy father's house"[2] and, blindfolded as we prisoners were, go down with me into the subterranean prison. Hear the cell door shut behind you. You are alone. All noise has ceased. Your only air supply comes to you through a pipe. If you feel the impulse to scream at the thought of being confined in such a place, just scream. The guards will soon put you in a strait-jacket. But "the King shall greatly desire thy beauty",[3] if you stay here as long as he has ordained for you.

Accept your thoughts of despair and of faith, your doubts and their solution, your moments of madness and their passing away. Allow it all to happen to you. You imagine that you are thinking. In fact, you are being thought. You may be an experiment for angels. You may be the object of a bet between God and Satan, like Job. Be determined only to cling to God, even if he slays you, even if he slays your faith. If you lose your faith, then remain faithlessly his. If all the fruits of the spirit disappear, and you remain a barren tree with only leaves, remember that leaves also have a purpose. Under their shadow, the fruitful ones may rest in the embraces of their Divine Lover. Leaves are used by the bride to make a garland for her beloved. Leaves are changed into healing medicines. And even when the leaves become yellow and fall withered to the ground, they can form a beautiful carpet on which he will walk towards those who, unlike you, have remained faithful to the end.

Go down into solitary confinement. I have brought you to the door of your cell. It is here that I disappear. You remain alone with him. It may be your bridal chamber. It may be a chamber of spiritual torture. I have to leave you. My place is in my own cell. You look at me and think you see madness in my face? I don't mind. Very soon, you will look like me. And perhaps you will be able to say to Jesus: "I am black, but comely."[4]

We have gone down into the darkness. Here you will experience the pressure, but also the rapture, of the great depths. At a great depth, things do not have the same colour as on the surface. Your sense of direction disappears. Your mind changes, supposing that you are able to keep your mind. You will probably wander off the right way.

May God help you! May God have mercy on all miserable sinners who pass through the rapture of the final depths.

R. W.

God's Unjust Laws

GOD

For years I have been preaching to men. I had almost forgotten that there is an invisible audience in church, too; that the angels are listening as we expound your word.

Now that I am alone with you, and with your invisible servants, I can begin a new series of sermons.

In church I had to be careful not to hurt the feelings or prejudices of my listeners. With you I can be absolutely frank. You have no inquisition. You will not try me for heresy. In front of other people I had to praise you. Here I am free to question you, and to reproach you, as David and Job and others have done.

I will tell you openly everything that is in my heart.

You have said: "It is not good that man should be alone."[1] And yet you are keeping me in solitary confinement. You created Eve to be with Adam. Yet you have taken away from me my wife. You are doing to me the very thing that you yourself have acknowledged to be wrong. How will you justify yourself when we meet? You will ask me why I have done things condemned by your word. It is surely far worse for a God not to fulfil his own word than for a man not to obey God's commandments. The judgment will be reciprocal. I can now understand the words of Isaiah: "Come now and let us reason *together*, saith the Lord."[2]

Jesus said: "The Father makes the sun to rise on the evil and on the good."[3] Our torturers are now at the beaches enjoying the sun. I have not seen it for months, being in a cell thirty feet under the earth. Jesus will ask me many things at the last judgment. That is his right. But I will ask him why the Father kept me without the sun. I am curious to know how he will answer me.

Ever since my conversion I have been intrigued by your word in Ezekiel: "I gave them also statutes that were not good and judgments whereby they should not live."[4] I have never heard a preacher explain this verse. The commentators also avoid it. Now I am beginning to understand something of this mystery.

No law can be righteous, even if it is divine, because every law fixes equal standards for men of unequal abilities, who are put in unequal situations.

This is true even of the ten commandments. "Thou shalt not make unto thee any graven image" is a law given equally to the man brought up in a strict puritan religion and the man with a long Catholic heritage. This law is not just, because the two men cannot fulfil it with the same ease. I once spoke to a Catholic about the second commandment, and he replied candidly: "Why are you Protestants so blind? The law says, 'Thou shalt not make *unto thee* any graven image.' This does not mean that Michelangelo or even a modest sculptor is not allowed to make one for you. It is only forbidden to individuals to make holy images, everyone according to his fancy. But the church is not forbidden to provide Christians with these means of inspiration."

I stared in amazement at this Catholic brother, who was not at all bothered by what worried me so much. He continued: "When God became incarnate in Jesus Christ, he took all the qualities of a man, including that of being a potential model for an object of art." And so on. I had never thought of it like that.

"Honour thy father and thy mother" is said to those whose fathers are saints and good men. But I have known people who reacted violently against this commandment. All they could remember was that their father was a drunkard and beat them unjustly, or that their mother had abandoned them. In my congregation I had a girl who had been raped by her father. Your law is not just. It commands us to honour every father, every mother, even the one who has bequeathed to me a criminal heredity. I have to honour my superiors in the church. Some of them have chosen martyrdom. Others have become stooges of the Communists. And I have to honour both categories. It is your law, but an unjust one.

"Thou shalt not kill" is said to a Swede or a Swiss whose nation has known no war for centuries. We, Rumanians, have the same commandment, although our country has been invaded by foreigners in every generation, and we have to defend ourselves.

"Thou shalt not steal" is said to a billionaire, who has more than he will ever need and has no reason to steal. I am terribly hungry, and would steal bread if only I could find it. But in doing this I would be breaking one of your unjust laws.

"Thou shalt not commit adultery" is said to a man who has a loving and beautiful wife who is a good sexual partner. But the law is also valid for the person who has an unbearable wife or husband, or none at all. How much John, one of our congregation, has suffered! He had a wife who had been sick for years and could not give him satisfaction. One unjust law after another.

"Thou shalt not bear false witness" is a law for the man who has no reason to lie, or perhaps is not even able to do so, not having the slightest imagination; it is also for me, who have to answer the Communist interrogator. If I tell him the truth, as he asks me, appealing to my Christian obligation, many other arrests will follow.

Rahab, after having hid the two Israelite spies, lied, saying that she did not know where they came from or where they had gone. Did she do wrong?

I remember that Spurgeon preached on this subject, and said that he had often tried to put himself in Rahab's place. Supposing he had hidden some persecuted Protestants and was asked by the authorities if they were in his house. What would his answer have been? It is known that he was very strict against lying. We had to lie in the Nazi times, too. So I was interested to read what he said: "I have tried to imagine what

I would say, and have never yet been able to make up my mind
. . . I have more light than Rahab, and certainly I have had
more leisure to consider the case, and yet I do not see my way.
I am not sure whether Rahab's lie was not more honest and
outspoken than many an evasion which has suggested itself to
very clever people."

I have often quoted his words to brethren who were worried
about having to lie to oppressing authorities. Spurgeon could
not make up his mind. I have made up mine. I lie to the
Communist examining officers, and I must say I do it with
delight.

"Let not your heart be troubled"[5] is said equally to the
chronic worrier and to the phlegmatic character who by his
nature is never anxious about anything. It is said to a well-to-
do American who has never known real trouble, and to my
prison-mate who has just tapped to me by morse code through
the wall that he is sentenced to death.

A law cannot help but be unjust. Even you, God, could not
avoid injustice once you started to make laws.

So your injustice is not only that you keep me alone in a
place without sun. The problem is a bigger one. You have
committed an injustice by placing men under laws in the first
place.

I will leave my personal problem with you. One way of
being free of something which worries you is to drown your
individual sorrow, which is only a drop, in the infinite ocean of
universal sorrow. But I put the general problem. Why did you
commit injustice towards mankind by giving us statutes which
you yourself acknowledge to be unjust?

You need Jesus, just as I need him. He is the Intercessor and
Mediator. I hear him every night interceding and mediating
for you, to make me understand and love you, just as he inter-
cedes with you on my behalf.

You needed his incarnation as much as I need it, though for
an altogether different reason. You have always known man
as he looks from the perspective of Godhead. But this does not
give you the whole truth. From the cell on the other side of me

a former judge tapped through the wall how he regrets all the prison sentences he has ever given. He passed sentence without knowing what it was to spend years in prison. You judged men without having lived as man and suffered and been tempted. You needed the experience of manhood. You were enriched by the experience of your Son becoming man. "Go forth, O ye daughters of Zion, and behold king Solomon with the crown wherewith his mother crowned him in the day of his espousals." [6] From eternity Christ has had all kinds of beautiful crowns. The most beautiful was given to him by his holy mother: the crown of being the God-man. He was poor, mocked, beaten, tempted. He died. Enriched by this experience, he returned to you. Now you can understand us much better.

You are a living God. To be alive means to evolve, to grow, to increase. A thing which always stays the same is not alive. The constant appeal in churches to "magnify the Lord" teaches us that you can be magnified – that is, made greater. Jesus made you greater.

From the experience of human life actually lived, Jesus Christ made the mystery of human life, as known from within, manifest in heaven.

On the other hand, he explains to us on earth, every night, the mystery of a God who gives laws which he himself acknowledges to be wrong.

.   .   .

There has been a pause in my speaking to you. It was not a rhetorical pause. In speaking with you such artifices are not necessary.

I paused because I was listening, just as in heaven the song of the seraphim is interrupted by moments of silence, when the smoke of the incense which comes with the prayers of the saints ascends up before you. [7]

I heard Christ explaining to me – **how** clearly his sheep distinguish his voice – that you gave us the law in the hope that we would not stop there but go beyond it, and so arrive at what you really intended.

One thing I am sure about now: your commandment is one thing, and your wish another.

You say, for example, that "vengeance is mine". You express that will to show your wrath, but you believe that our faith will be big enough to stay your hand when you desire to avenge yourself. Yes, we will prevent you, even if you command us to the contrary. A good sheepdog does not easily stop barking at a stranger even if the shepherd orders it.

I once spoke harshly to my son, reproving him for some wrongdoing. He did not look me in the face, and I asked him why. He answered: "I am not looking at your mouth which is speaking the bitter words but at your loving heart from which they flow." So we are not meant to look at the strict words of your commandments but at the loving intentions with which they were given.

David knew all your laws about animal sacrifices, but he said: "Sacrifice and offering thou didst not desire." [8] The Jews had got from the Egyptians the wrong ideas about gods who always expect us to give them something. Jehovah, to warn them against bringing human sacrifices as other people did, ordered them to stop at a lamb or a pigeon. But David guessed that new life begins when a man understands that it is you who sacrificed the one whom you most love. You don't expect us to take life in order to become pleasant in your eyes.

One of your most unrighteous laws is about the cities of refuge. [9]

If someone killed unintentionally and the kinsmen of the victim wanted vengeance you ordered the murderer to flee to a city of refuge. Suppose that several men are guilty of such a murder, but one cannot run as fast as the others. Not everyone can run uphill at the same speed. The one who runs well reaches the city of refuge and is safe, although he is as guilty as his comrade, whereas the slower man is killed by the avenger.

Can righteousness depend on the speed at which a man can move his legs?

This unrighteousness is perpetuated in the New Testament, where it is said that those who overcome will receive their reward. And what of those who are defeated by sin, although they longed for holiness?

Love will always lose the prize, according to the law, because love is always beaten in the race. Only evil and vice can make the records. Love is always late.

Jesus teaches us this in the parable of the good Samaritan.

Did the three men make a wager as to who would travel fastest from Jerusalem to Jericho? They were a Jewish priest, a Levite and a Samaritan.

All three started at the same time. The priest and the Levite were ambitious, and hurried on because they wanted to win the wager and gain fame. They heard groans from someone wounded and in pain; somebody cried for help. Because they were good men, they felt compassion for him; as they ran, they said a prayer for the wounded man, but they did not stop because there was a prize and fame to be had at the end of the race. Besides, the place was dangerous. There were rumours of bandits around.

The Samaritan was quite a different sort of man. One wonders why he entered into the wager. For him, the most important thing was not the money, nor the fame, but love for every living thing. When he heard the groans, he stooped down, anointed the wounded man and took him to an inn, which lay in the direction from which he had come. So he lost the race, as love always does.

"I am sick of love," says the bride.[10] The sick cannot win races; they cannot overcome. Jesus said that the Kingdom of Heaven is taken by violence.[11] But love has no strength to commit violence. It is easy for a great sinner to force the gate of heaven. Saints and loving characters have to rely on grace more than the others in order to be saved, because they can do the least for themselves.

It is unjust for the law to demand the same swiftness and victories from everyone.

I understand now why I have to wait so long in prison for my Bridegroom to come. I am sure he has left his place to come to help us, but he stops at every wounded person along his way. Jairus implored him for his daughter who was dying, but Jesus found a sick woman on the way, and so he allowed Jairus' daughter to die in the meantime.[12]

Who knows if Jesus, coming to our rescue, has not met on his way a flower whose petals were burdened with drops of dew, and stopped to straighten them out?

I am sick of love, and so I cannot do your works. You are love itself, and therefore sickness itself. You cannot come in time to give me back to my family, although you know that "it is not good for man to be alone". You are sick of love, and cannot make the sun rise for me, too. Who knows what sheep fallen into a ditch you had to help, Father, when Jesus was on Golgotha. So he had to remain without a ray of light and without a drop of water.

I cannot fulfil your law. Through Jesus you have released me from this obligation.

You have all the handicaps of love and cannot fulfil your many promises to be my helper. But I also release you from all obligations towards me taken by covenant, as you release me from all your statutes. They are not good. They are simply generalities. For you I am unique, as you are for me.

And we will pass together the years of solitary confinement, satisfied with loving and being loved. I will not reproach you for your evil statutes and unjust laws. You will not reproach me for having broken them.

How glad I am that for the first time I have been able to speak so openly with you. So, in the end, I realise that you have not left me alone. I am with you. Neither have you left me without the sun. I see the sun of righteousness rising in my dark cell.

Thanks and praise. *Amen*.

A Christian Encounters
Gabriel

DEAR BROTHERS AND SISTERS

I cannot see you, but I will preach to you from a distance.

I have several times experienced what is called extra-sensory perception. Here is one example.

A Russian lady officer was converted in our home. Then she went away with her regiment towards Hungary and Austria, and I did not hear from her again. Meanwhile, we moved into another house. One morning, just at the busiest time, I felt an irresistible impulse to return to my former apartment, although I had nothing to do there. When I approached the house I saw coming towards it from the other direction that Russian sister. She was passing through Bucharest on her way home to Stalingrad. Between trains she had some hours to spare, and she had prayed with all her heart that I would be at home so that she might get some further instruction in Christianity. Had I not been there just at that moment the unique opportunity would have been lost.

I could quote many other such instances.

You also may be capable of such perception at a distance. The prophets of old spoke to men far away. "Pass ye away, thou inhabitant of Saphir . . . O thou inhabitant of Lachish . . . I will bring an heir unto thee, O inhabitant of Mareshah . . . thou, Bethlehem Ephratah," said Micah in one and the same speech,[1] being sure that the angels would bring his words to distant cities.

So I am sure that my words, uttered in a solitary cell, will reach at least some of you, those who have the rare virtue of being silent and listening.

I will share with you some of the spiritual experiences

through which we pass in our underground prison. Although everyone is alone in a cell we communicate with each other by tapping messages in code through the wall. So I happen to know the following events.

It was ten o'clock at night. We always know exactly when it is ten o'clock. With chronometric exactitude at this hour the great tortures begin. In the mornings you can get a heavy beating. But the tortures are reserved for this dark hour. You can hear the screams. The acoustics in the arched corridors are such that the wailings bounce off one wall and on to another with ever-increasing volume. At the first cry, the signal is given through the wall from one cell to the other, three knocks reminding us that we must begin our spiritual exercises; first, the examination of conscience, judging all our attitudes, thoughts and actions of the past day. A Jesuit priest taught us all to do this.

The Christian about whom I speak to you today did not have a very high regard for such self-examination. He considered that conscience is not so much the voice of God in us as the voice of our social environment. An action which would produce great remorse in one Christian is considered morally justified by another who comes from a different background. Conscience judges us according to its own law. But laws are generalisations, and do not take into account individual abilities and circumstances. You may be the staunchest Protestant and believe in salvation by faith alone. The conscience is always Catholic and tortures you with the remembrance of your actions, as if our relationship with God depended on these.

Conscience knows nothing about causality. It does not accept determinism. It believes in the fallacy of free will. It does not acknowledge the obvious fact that my action was the unavoidable result of my character, shaped by my whole past life, and the only response which I, as a unique personality, could give to external stimulants. Conscience attributes to me alone the guilt of an action which was the end result of the influence of thousands of other people: ancestors who transmitted to me a certain heredity; teachers and parents who gave me a faulty education; authors, actors, friends and enemies who moulded my soul; the pressure of my social environment; and so on.

Conscience knows nothing about God's plans in which my sinful act may have played a necessary role – "Against thy holy child Jesus, whom thou hast anointed, both Herod and Pontius Pilate with the Gentiles and the people of Israel were gathered together, for to do whatsoever thy hand and thy counsel determined before to be done."[2]

Conscience is biased. When you examine yourself about everything you have done during the day, it will remind you only of the bad things. The good it forgets. And it only distinguishes between black and white. It does not know about the grey – the necessity, imposed sometimes by the circumstances of life, to choose not between good and evil but between two evils.

Conscience does not accept the words of St. Philip Neri that we must not expect to become saints in four days. The best it can do, after much doubt and torment, is to accept the remission of sins, that is, pardon for guilt. The highest doctrine of the Bible, the one about justification, according to which we appear before God absolutely free from guilt, is completely unacceptable to conscience. It is totally unable to grasp the truth that not only the sinner but also the sin can become as white as snow.[3]

I would not like to abolish conscience, as Hitler did, calling it a Jewish invention. The results of that were horrible. Conscience has an enormous social value. A tender conscience gives you a right attitude to your fellow-men. But God does not love you more after a good deed or less after a bad one.

Self-examination always leaves you sad. You compare what you have done with what Jesus would have done in similar circumstances, and bitterly reproach yourself. But to ask what Jesus would have done in similar circumstances is as reasonable as to ask how far a snail would have gone during a day if it had been a hare. It is a snail and not a hare. And I am I. I am not Jesus. To act like Jesus I would have to be God incarnate, born of a holy virgin. I would have to have his education. I would have to have angels at my disposal. I would have to possess his miraculous power. I would have to be a prophet, and a carpenter of two thousand years ago in Palestine.

Luther warned men of the great sin of sadness. He said that it is better for a Christian to be drunk than to be sad. The Communists have tortured us enough. Why should we torture ourselves? Luther said again that remorse before Calvary is of God; remorse after you have been to Calvary is of the devil. Repent of your sin, yes; but do not make your sin a subject for long and melancholy meditation. Why should I cheat God by spending my time and energy on remorse? I am greater than my sins. Conscience would try to identify me with them.

Our brother did not care for these torturings of the soul. The Talmud says: "The sun has set and the day is clear." When the signal was given each night our brother would prepare to dance to the glory of God.

Before the signal was given he lay on his bed. Like the ticking of a watch, in every pulse beat of his heart there was a thought about Jesus. His longing after the Bridegroom was a burning fire. He whispered "Jesus" at every breath. And now the signal came. It was time to begin his holy – or perhaps his crazy – dance.

While he was dancing he heard an angel say: "Hail, Gheorghe, full of grace. God is with thee. Blessed art thou." The brother had been brought up in respect for the traditions of the early desert fathers. He knew what to do in such cases. He asked the angel: "To whom are you sent?" The angel answered: "To you, Gheorghe." The Christian answered: "There are many others with the name of Gheorghe around me in other cells. You have come to the wrong one. I am not worthy to hear the voice of angels." His circling round became even crazier to drive away the temptation. The dance was a sacrifice on the altar of God.

But the angel – it was Gabriel – remained. How insistent angels are! Then something was conceived in this Christian, as in Mary in times past (or perhaps he only then discovered what had long been there). There quickened in this Christian the germ of a new life which would give him in the future the power to overcome where he had been defeated in times past. He knew now that he would be able to bear things more painful than death, even the worst of mockeries.

Since that experience, that Christian lives no more. Christ lives in him. He lives only to nurture this new life, to raise up in all good the author of all virtue. What a responsibility! As with Mary, it is his task to bring to maturity the very king of heaven.

This Christian feels it is his special task to make Jesus a man of the twentieth century – or rather of the twenty-first century; to make him a modern intellectual – or rather, the one who will show the modern intellectuals the path ahead. His task is to make him a man who will weep in our generation as he wept in Jerusalem two thousand years ago; to make him today's man of sorrows.

Jesus is for ever weeping.

There is an ancient legend which says that, when Jesus was a child, Joseph loved him so much that he would never come home from the market without bringing him some toy or candy. The little Jesus was so used to this that, whenever Joseph went to town, the child would wait by the window to see when he returned. Then he would run to meet him and ask him: "Father, what have you brought me?" Once, Joseph had no money and came home empty-handed. When Jesus ran to meet him and put the usual question, Joseph replied, discouraged: "Nothing." Then the child began to weep bitterly. And, seeing this, Joseph began to weep too.

The holy virgin came out of the house and saw both of them in tears. She asked what was wrong. When Joseph explained, she said, amazed: "I can understand why he is weeping. He is only a child. But why are you in tears?" Joseph answered: "The weeping of Jesus has a deep meaning. This child will always sit at the windows of heaven waiting for his beloved ones to return. He will run to meet each one, asking him, 'What have you brought me?' And if the answer is, like mine, 'Nothing,' he will weep in heaven as you see him weeping now."

The Christian of whom I am speaking feels it to be his task to actualise these tears. As in times past Jesus wept over Jerusalem, so he will weep now over Moscow, which kills the prophets and stones those who are sent to it. He will weep over Berlin, capital of a great nation which cannot be unified. He will weep over Oslo and Stockholm, towns with empty churches. He will weep over London and Washington, which have sacrificed one-third of the world into the hands of the Communist torturers who have just beaten a woman. I can hear her heart-rending cries.

Jesus is now living in the heart of this Christian. Those who do not have Jesus, or who have only a ghost (that is, the Jesus of two thousand years ago), will mock this man who is a present-day Mary. They say the rosary endlessly – "Hail, Mary, full of grace," meaning always the Mary of old, and remaining blind to a Mary of today.

But this Christian has met Gabriel. He has lived in the reality of the mystical union. Christ has been conceived in him. *Amen.*

The Mother of the Lord

DEAR BROTHERS AND SISTERS

We live on very little. A rich child with many toys is bored with them. A child in the slums has a box, and pushes it around. He calls it a car, a wagon, an engine. He has a stick and rides on it, and calls it a horse.

So we live on little things, but enrich them by our imagination.

Our telegraph through the wall functions perfectly. In the fourth cell to my right is a girl, from the Underground church, who has been severely tortured but does not betray. She is only eighteen. Her name is Mary.

This communication started in me a series of thoughts which I wish to share with you.

Mary – what a holy name!

Primitive peoples have always had their goddesses as well as their gods. They have, in a distorted form, a basically sound intuition, or perhaps something of the primary revelation has remained with them. There is a female principle in Godhead. Scholars who are privileged to study the Holy Scriptures in the original languages, know that *"ruah"*, the Hebrew word for "spirit" is a feminine noun. In Genesis 1, if you translate literally you must read: "And the Spirit of God moved in a feminine manner (*merahefet*) upon the face of the waters." In Aramaic, the language spoken by Jesus, the word for spirit is also feminine – *"ruha"*.

The angel who appeared to Joseph in a dream told him that his bride, Mary, "shall bring forth a son, and thou shalt call his name 'Jesus' " (in Hebrew "Jeshuah", again a feminine word). It is as though we were to call a boy Helen or Katherine.

A man with a female name. It was this mystery which was expressed in the outward appearance of an Orthodox priest: he had to have a beard, but wear a woman's robe.

Whenever I feel God near me in this solitary cell I always have the impression that there is also a female presence. St. John the Evangelist, in conditions similar to mine, alone, exiled on Patmos, saw God sitting on the throne. "And he that sat was to look upon like a jasper and a sardine stone."[1] But there also appeared to him in heaven what was to him a great wonder, as it was to me: "a woman clothed with the sun and the moon under her feet and upon her head a crown of twelve stars".[2] Commentators make all kinds of guesses as to who this woman might be. We have the explanation in the very beginning of the Bible: "God created man in his own image, in the image of God created he him; male and female created he them."[3] This is the image of God: male and female. So there is a female principle in Godhead. The Kabbala calls it "the Matrona". God has all the perfections; he cannot be limited to the male ones.

When I was arrested under the Nazis, I saw prisoners being taken out to exercise in the prison yard. Each one was handcuffed behind his back, and they were chained one to another, so that they had to walk in a circle. A Catholic priest, noticing this, exclaimed: "A human rosary!" And, as he had no beads, he said his "Hail, Marys", seeing every man chained to him as a knot in the rosary.

An incident like this can move the heart of a Protestant, too.

I would never consent to call Mary "Queen of heaven", "Leader of the angelic hosts", "Queen of the Church", "Queen of mankind" and so on, because I would not like to leave God unemployed. But my love and reverence for her has certainly increased with my experiences in prisons.

And now, when I hear about the tortured Mary near me, my thoughts go to the mother of the Lord.

The genealogy of Jesus, as recounted by Matthew, gives forty-two generations from Abraham to Christ. But count them and you will find that only forty-one are enumerated, including Christ. St. Matthew was a publican. So we may presume that he knew how to count. Why did he list forty-one and say that there are forty-two? If this was a simple error, how is it that it has been perpetrated for twenty centuries? You can see that St. Matthew wished to hide a mystery by the fact that he really pretends to give forty-two names by a cunning device. He has three sets of fourteen names each. He repeats the name of Jechonias, the last in the second series, as the first in the third, so that the inattentive reader may never observe that one of the alleged forty-two is missing. Who is this missing forty-second link?

Another biblical curiosity: nearly all the women of the Gospels are named Mary. We have Mary, the holy virgin; Mary Magdalene; Mary of Bethany; Mary the mother of James and Joseph; Mary the wife of Cleopas; and one simply called "the other Mary". This makes six. If we had one Mary more, we would have the holy number seven. Is one Mary missing?

By the cross there stood only Marys, four of them. The relevant Bible verse sounds very strange: "There stood by the cross of Jesus his mother and his mother's sister, Mary."[4] But the mother's name was Mary. Two sisters don't have the same name.

What if Mary (in Hebrew Miriam, "the star of the sea", the star which shows the way to those who sail on the ocean of spirituality) is not used in the Bible as a name only? It seems that it was also a title given to a certain type of Christian woman in the early church, as the Communists call each other "comrade", and as there are titles in the army and in masonry.

So anybody can become a Mary, just as anybody can become a comrade, or a major in the army.

A third mystery: Jesus said, "Whosoever shall do the will of my Father which is in heaven, the same is my brother and my sister, and mother."[5] He is the first-born among many brethren. It is easy to understand what it means to hold him in the relationship of a brother. But how can one become his mother? He says that this is possible, too.

It is a great privilege to be God's child, but how much greater a privilege to have God as one's child! Jesus tells us that this is possible for us. Nestorius fought against calling Mary "Theotokos" (the one who gives birth to God), but a general council of the church defeated him. Christ is God. And Mary held God as a baby in her arms. She washed him, she cared for him, she fed him, she brought him up. Her God was dependent upon her. She is unique as the first and the greatest mother of God. But this experience is not entirely reserved for her. Jesus says that the one who fulfils his will can be his mother, can be with him in the relationship which a mother has towards her child.

What does all this mean?

The highest form of love is that of a mother for her child. The child's love towards its mother contains a grain of interest; it turns to its mother for every need. The child's love towards its father is similar: Father gives the pocket money. In every human love some kind of interest is mixed. Only a mother's love is totally self-sacrificing. She gives everything for her children, expecting nothing in return.

Mary, the mother of God, gave everything for Jesus and never received anything from him, not even good words. After the resurrection, when he showed himself to so many, comforting their sad hearts, he did not show himself to his mother. There was a purpose in this. He offered her, by this, the highest opportunity: to give to God without claiming ever to receive anything in return.

Those who have attained this spiritual position bear the title of a "Mary". I think that this should be the sense of the Catholic word "marianite". Then Protestants could not object.

And now we come back to the one missing link in the genealogy of Jesus. This genealogy is not history. Even a superficial comparison with the genealogy of the Jewish kings in the Old Testament, and with the one in St. Luke, is sufficient to show that they do not agree. The genealogy of Jesus according to St. Matthew is not a historical succession, but a ladder of initiation.

You begin by identifying yourself with Abraham, the father

of all the faithful; you pass through the experience of Isaac sacrificed by his father, as Christians in our country have to deprive their children of a happy childhood in order to remain faithful to Christ. You then become Jacob, who saw the angels ascending and descending, to teach him that in the spiritual life you cannot stop at any point. If you do not advance, you slide back. God is at the top of the ladder. Sweet communion with him in the highest sense of the word is possible only there. You continue the initiation, reliving the lives of Judah and all the others until you arrive at the stage of Mary, of being towards God as a mother is towards her child. The Mary of two thousand years ago gave birth to Jesus Christ, the historical person of whom the Gospels speak.

But you too can have your meeting with the archangel Gabriel. Christ can be conceived in your heart, as a result of the forty preceding experiences of communion with saints, common men and sinners of all the ages. You can be a Mary with self-sacrificing love, which wishes only to give, not asking anything in exchange. The Christ in you, the hope of glory, will be the forty-second person in the chain. Your aim will have been accomplished.

You will concentrate on one thing, to serve God who is your child. You will not depart from this, not even when the Communists tempt you with their promises of release if you betray; not even when you are tortured.

Hail, Mary, my beloved sister in the fourth cell; hail, Mary, full of grace. God is with you. Blessed are you among women, and blessed is the fruit of your heart. And whence is this to me, that the mother of my Lord should sit near me in a royal prison cell? For lo, as soon as the tapping through the wall of the cell gave me knowledge of your presence and of your faithfulness, my babe leapt in my heart for joy.

God help us all to arrive at the final, missing link in St. Matthew's genealogy. *Amen.*

Duty Never Ends

DEAR BROTHERS AND SISTERS

St. Paul could write letters when he was in prison. He had ink and parchment. St. John, too, could write to the churches from his exile on Patmos.

We have no paper and no ink. But there is one way of writing which they cannot forbid us: to write with the Spirit on the hearts of men, even if they are far from us.

I may as well teach you the technique of this kind of writing, so that you may be able to use it too.

A technique in matters of the Spirit? Usually, Christians are very vague in thinking and speaking about spiritual matters. But there are laws of the Spirit just as there are laws of the material world. It is possible to orientate yourself in the spiritual world, just as you do in the material world. The seers of old knew not only that they had met an angel, but what legion he belonged to, and what his name was – Michael or Gabriel. When you know the laws of the Spirit, you can use a certain technique, just as a technique in material things becomes possible when you know the natural laws.

The basic principles of writing with the Spirit in the hearts of men far away are these:

1. Don't think about the man on whom you wish to concentrate in order to convey to him a message from God, except in the hour of that concentration. Don't speak about him. He should be out of your mind. Then all your potential of interest and love for him, which would otherwise be dissipated, will be available in the hour of concentration. I tell myself jokes and play chess with myself and hum all kinds of melodies before I concentrate on speaking to you.

2. Meditation must precede the delivery of the message. I must think the message through, and refine it to contain, in the most condensed form, what I consider to be essential for you to know. I must meditate about how the knowledge of this message from God might beautify your soul; what loss it could be for you not to know exactly the state of heart of your brothers and sisters in jail, you being one soul with them, their sufferings and doubts and victories being yours.

3. From meditation I must pass to contemplation. I must see you with my spiritual eyes as I used to see you in church. I must recognise every face. You must be as real to me as if I were actually seeing your picture. More than this, I must see you laughing or weeping according to what I tell you. Meditation calls for burning love; contemplation requires an exercise of the imagination. We can all evoke a loved one in our daydreams. Exercise this faculty, and you will be able to write in the Spirit.

4. Actually write with letters your message on the hearts of those whom you now have before you in the spirit. At first, it is best to make the gestures with your hand, as if you were actually inscribing the words.

5. Never allow the mental pictures of those to whom you are writing to disappear from your view until you can see on their faces that they have understood your message. There should be a nod, a smile or a shake of the head. But there should be a reaction.

All prisoners, and pastors and Christians of the Underground church should learn this forgotten art, as the possibilities of normal communication become less and less.

In the end, prayer is also something like writing with the Spirit on the heart of God. And the technique of real prayer is something like that I have just described, the face which the Christian has before him being that of Jesus Christ.

But it was not really about this that I wished to speak to you today. I have something else to tell you.

I have observed that Jesus and the angels, listening to my sermons delivered in the solitary cell, enjoy particularly the stories which illustrate them. Just as my son Mihai used to beg me: "Tell me that story again," I have the feeling that they too would like to ask me to repeat a story.

So I will tell you a story:

A young king was quarrelsome and gave no peace to the wise old king of a neighbouring country. The old king entreated for friendly relations, but in vain. The young king started a war. The old king, remembering how many foolish things he himself had done in his youth, and that there is an age from which we cannot expect wisdom, gave orders to his officers to capture his young enemy alive.

So it was done. He was brought in chains before the victor. The old man pitied the youngster, but pretended to be very angry with him and sentenced him to death. The young king begged for his life. So the old man told him: "I will give you a chance. Tomorrow you will be given a jug of water, full to the brim. You must carry it from one end of the main street of the city to the other, without spilling a drop. If you do not succeed, your life is lost."

The next day the procession started – the prisoner with the jug of water; around him soldiers to guard him; behind him the executioner with his axe, a terrifying reminder that he would be beheaded on the spot if he failed. The old king had given orders that on one side of the street there should be a mob to boo the prisoner, on the other side a crowd to cheer him.

The prisoner succeeded. He did not spill a drop. The old king asked him: "When so many people were mocking you, did you answer them back?" The young man answered: "I had no time for that. I had to be careful about my jug." "But did you thank the ones who cheered you?" "What business had I with them? Their acclamation could not help me. I was concerned with my jug of water."

The old king set him free with this advice: "You have been entrusted with a soul. You have to bring it back to the Lord whole and clean. That is the only thing that counts. If you do not succeed, you perish. Don't seek the applause of men by cheap victories. Don't worry if they mock you. Watch over your soul."

The tick-tock of the pendulum in the prison corridor makes me conscious that time passes here, as it passes for those who are free. Soon I will have to give an account of every second of my life. Today is my fortieth birthday. I have to account for 1,261,440,000 seconds. While I was making this calculation, other seconds have passed. I have a duty to fulfil every second. The fact that I am in solitary confinement does not release me from this duty.

As a rule, prisoners pass their time in trifles. I know this from my time in the Nazi prison. If they are not compelled to do slave labour, they tell each other stories and jokes. Sometimes they quarrel. They waste their time, just as some millionaires do.

Millionaires use a lot, prisoners very little, of nature's wealth, without always feeling it their duty to give something to the world.

In prison there is a feeling of being released from duty, especially when you are in solitary confinement. Who has the right to ask anything from you when you are in such terrible circumstances?

But the imperative of life knows no excuses. Duty is a categorical demand, whether you are in happiness or unhappiness. Mocked, hungry, jailed, sick, falsely charged, tortured, alone, you have to serve the Highest.

I know my duty. It does not consist so much in doing things. Prison conditions hinder me from accomplishing deeds. Duty consists mostly in becoming something. "I am what I am" is the usual translation of what God said to Moses. A more literal rendering of the Hebrew "*Ehjeh asher ehjeh*" is "I will become what I will become". He himself is constantly becoming something. This is my duty too. My duty is to become more and more myself. When God formed me in the hidden place, he made me to be myself, to be in my own way the herald of his glory, to be unique, as God himself is unique.

To be yourself is much more than being truthful, or loving,

or religious, because your self contains all these and much more. Jesus was not content to be the truth alone. Truth was too little a thing for him. Hitler said: "Truth is an oft-repeated lie." That is nonsense. But if we take the classical definition of the word, "truth is correspondence between reality and our thoughts", what about the realities which are incomprehensible to us, which we don't even know? Jesus did not wish to be truth alone. He is truth and way and life. He did not wish to be love alone. He knows how to hate, too. He said to the church at Ephesus: "This thou hast, that thou hatest the deeds of the Nicolaitans, which I also hate."[1]

The Hebrew word for truth is *"emeth"*. It is written with the first, the middle and the last letters of the alphabet. But reality has no beginning and no end. Reality is greater than truth. The Greek word for truth is *alethia*, which means, etymologically, "nothing forgotten". But there is something more than *alethia*; there is the forgetting, too.

Truth belongs to the conscious part of our being, a little island in the ocean of the unconscious. Love is one among many human feelings. Jesus is more than truth and love. Myths belong to him as much as the truth. So they have a powerful meaning for me.

I have to become myself, a self not imprisoned in a set pattern, as my body is imprisoned in this cell.

I must become the greatest being that I can become here on earth; "I will become what I will become", taking as my final goal Jesus, who did so.

Then I will be able to fulfil an outward duty even here.

And what if I am tortured? Christ saved a robber while he was on the cross. My brethren to my right and left have sometimes brought their torturers to Christ. A Communist officer, beating a Christian prisoner with a rubber truncheon, put his stick aside and asked: "What is it about you? How is it that your face is shining? You have something like a halo round your head. How can you look at me so lovingly? I would never love a man who jailed and beat me. How is it that you can obey the foolish commandment of your Christ to love your enemy?" The Christian answered: "I am not obeying a commandment. It is not that I love you only because Jesus orders me to. Jesus has given me a new heart and a new character. If I wanted to hate you, I would no longer be able to do so. A nightingale cannot sound like a crow, because it is a nightingale and not a crow. So a Christian can only love." That rubber truncheon has remained put aside for ever.

We are in hell. Sometimes, during nights of horror, I look at the cup of water which is in my cell. Only this assures me that it is not the eternal hell. There the damned have no water. But even in hell you are not released from duty. How often I have said the words of the creed: "He descended into hell." He descended to enrich the tormented souls with the gifts of God.

That is what we are doing. We bring souls to Christ by tapping the gospel through the wall.

The important thing is always to have one aim, and to pursue it in stormy and fair weather. Jesus wants our eyes to be single.[2] The Hebrew language did not have the word "intention". Jesus, using these words, meant that our intention should be single: to be the highest we can be, and then not to worry any more. Man always does what he is; he reacts to outward circumstances according to his character.

The Romans had a proverb: "*Quod agis, agi*" (do what you do), do just one thing. Most of us, when we are praying, think of the pancake on the fire which might burn. While making pancakes, we think how nice it would be to pass our time in prayer. While speaking with one man, we think how useful it would be to pass our time with another. We never do anything well. Only one thing can be done well at a time. Those who participate in too many sports never become champions.

Our earthly life is short. Let us not be like the ass in the story who, having two heaps of hay before him, died of hunger, not knowing which to choose. But let us concentrate upon our single aim: to develop a heavenly character, which by contagion will fill God's heaven with men. *Amen.*

Samson in Prison

DEAR BROTHERS AND SISTERS

I used to consider those of my fellow-prisoners who are in prison for their belief as martyrs. But communicating with them through the wall (and the telegraph is functioning through many cells to my right and my left), I discovered that none of them were conscious of being martyrs. They felt that God was punishing them for their sins. Even St. Paul, who suffered so much for his faith, called himself "the chief of sinners".[1]

And I think they are right. We must distinguish between the appearance and the substance, between what people call "facts" or "truth" and their spiritual significance.

Who can work as a conspirator in the Underground church and always speak what is generally called "truth"? When I introduced myself, I did it under a cover-name. The one with whom I was speaking might be an informer. If asked by someone where I was yesterday, a factually correct answer might bring many people into great trouble. Today again the interrogator told me: "You are a Christian and a pastor. Your religion obliges you to tell us the whole truth." I had my own thoughts about this. If I had complied with his demands, other brethren would have been arrested.

Nobody can be a leader in the Underground church without re-evaluating the notion of truth.

So, to come back to the problem of martyrs. To outward appearance, anyone who has been killed or imprisoned for his convictions is a martyr. But the substance may be otherwise. God may use the Communists to punish you for a sin. He can lead them to put you in a solitary cell because he wishes to deal better with your soul.

How offended the Jews must have been by Jesus when they told him about some Galileans whose blood Pilate had mingled with their sacrifices.[2] Now these were surely martyrs of the Mosaic faith and for the national cause. The Jews had a deep respect for men like these who had died *"al kidush hashem"*, for the glory of the Name. But Jesus called the slaughtered Galileans simply "sinners".

He looked at the substance. Sinners – that is what even martyrs are before God. Luther makes a distinction between "sinners of the left" and "sinners of the right", between scoundrels and law-abiding men who observe the religious commandments, even that of self-sacrifice, in order to earn paradise. Both types of men are sinners.

I am nothing else than a sinner. I have never known a man worse than me. The One who can free me prefers to keep me in prison as a punishment for my transgression. Samson was in prison because he had sinned, although the Philistines had jailed him because of his noble fight for the Mosaic cause. I am a sinner, but I know that if I accept my punishment with whole-hearted humility, my strength will grow.

Like all the other prisoners, I had my hair cut short until today. Now they announce that I am to be allowed to let it grow, a sure sign that I shall soon be brought before the court. They make you look a little bit more human before presenting you to the judges. The hair will grow very slowly in this sub-terranean cell, in which never a ray of sun enters. But still it will grow. This made me think about Samson. His strength grew simultaneously with his hair.

I will become an embodiment of power, and will be able to slay more Philistines at my death than I slew in my whole Christian life. I will kill them, even if I die with them.

Once this power has come back, I will no longer wish for my release. This age has produced powers unknown in the past. But I will draw from God the still unknown powers of the ages to come, the hidden spiritual powers. Though they remain behind prison walls, those who possess this power can demolish temples and build them again. They can remain in a dark cell, and yet make the sun shine in many hearts. They can be sad and depressed, yet fill many souls with gladness.

How I would like to become what Samson became in prison!

True worship is not that on Mount Gerizim, the place of the Samaritan temple, nor that in Jerusalem. True worship is to grow in power to destroy everything which opposes the One crucified for me.

Sin is every second of my life spent on something other than the destruction of what opposes the triumph of love.

There are not certain deeds which are sinful under all circumstances, and other deeds which are always good. The mud with which we are all smeared contains in its mixture many compassionate actions.

Charity given to a drunkard, who after having drunk liquor with your money, beats his wife, is sin. Judith, on the other hand, killed. So did Jael.[3] But they freed the world from tyrants. Around me, in the other cells, are many patriots who have killed. It was for the sake of freedom. It is foolish to consider that knitting a pullover for some lazy man is a good deed, while the attempt of German generals to stop the slaughter of millions of innocent victims by killing Hitler is to be despised as murder.

For me, the only criterion of a deed is: does it prepare the way for the final triumph of love, or not?

We have to choose between good as the means, and good as the end. If I am always good towards all men, even those who by deceit and terror hinder the victory of love, good will never triumph. The wicked will profit by my meekness, and consolidate the position of evil. If I choose good as my goal, I have to commit many actions which are condemned as evil in the moral catalogue of the world.

The Bible writes about God sending enticing spirits.[4] So I have no scruples about using untruth to lead astray my interrogators. My only scruple is in having scruples about such an attitude.

God praised those who killed Sisera, Agag, Holofernes. The same words are used in the Bible about Jael, who killed Sisera, as are used by the archangel to the holy virgin: "Blessed above women shall Jael, the wife of Heber the Kenite be, blessed shall she be above women in the tent." [5] This, because she smote an enemy of God. In one of the cells on this corridor is Nina, a Rumanian girl, who did something similar. If it was right to kill a foreign oppressor several thousands of years ago, it must be right now also. The New Testament praises such heroes of the Old Testament. The Jewish people had to be defended. The Rumanian people have the same right.

The same Spirit of God who inspired 1 Corinthians 13, the poem of love, inspired the book of Esther, in which the enemies of God are ruthlessly destroyed. The Holy Spirit has arranged for both to be part of the same holy book. What is more, the first Christians had as their only holy Scriptures the scrolls of the Old Testament. The New Testament was written decades later, and completed towards the end of the first century.

God has brought together poems of love and books which teach determination to uproot the enemy, in order to perfect us and give us only one aim: to cause love to triumph at last. Bloody fighting against tyrants must work together with acts of tender charity towards the attaining of this aim.

We must set ourselves in our life the highest aim, to be his servants and the servants of all. Then "good" or "evil" deeds will have the same result, to bring love to triumph.

The question is a very real one for me. Christians around me have participated in the patriotic fight against the Communist oppressor and have had to kill. They tap their confessions through the wall. But was their action sin? Would I take part in such a fight?

In Dostoievsky's *The Brothers Karamazov*, Ivan says, in effect: "It is not God that I don't accept, understand this, it is the world that he has created, the divine world which I do not accept, and cannot agree to accept . . . I am as convinced as a child that . . . at last, in the world finale, at the moment of eternal harmony, something so precious will happen and appear that it will be enough . . . to expiate all people's crimes . . . but I don't accept it, and I don't want to . . . I would rather remain with unavenged suffering . . . And besides, they make the harmony too expensive, we cannot afford to pay quite so much to enter. That is why I am hurrying to return my entrance ticket. If I am an honest man, I am obliged to return it as far in advance as possible. That is what I am doing. It is not God I don't accept, Alyosha, I am only returning the ticket to him in the most respectful manner."

Ivan goes on to say to Alyosha: "Tell me frankly yourself, I am asking you, so answer: Imagine that you yourself are erecting the edifice of human destiny with the purpose of making people happy in the finale and giving them, at last, peace and quiet, but that to do so it is necessary and inevitable to torture just one tiny creature, that same little child who beats his chest with his little fist, and base this edifice on his unavenged little tears, would you consent to be the architect on these conditions? Tell me and don't lie."

"No, I wouldn't," Alyosha said softly.

My answer is: "I would." This was Abraham's answer. He was ready to sacrifice his own child for this. His followers know that the five octillions of atoms which constitute the body of the child are the shrine of a spirit, perhaps the prison cell of a spirit, and that the spirit will be happy to have got rid of it. They believe what the *Bhagavad Gita* says, that the killer may be no more than the fulfiller of God's predestination for a man. It is right, when necessary, to kill for the sake of freedom, of fatherland, of God. If it is sacred history when the Jews fought against tyrants, why should the fight of Rumanians to get rid of Communist slavery not be sacred also?

No, you have not sinned, patriotic fighters.

St. Augustine said: "Love God, and do what you will."

It is written: "Sing unto the Lord a new song."[6] This is a warrior's song. Nobody is so courageous a warrior as the Lord himself. He never slumbers nor sleeps. Christianity teaches us not so much to be good as to be warriors for the good. You cannot be a warrior for the good without fighting, and so striking not only abstract evil and evil institutions but also evil men.

God is the beginning and the end. The middle of the day is ours. We do not know what the future holds for us. And I do not want his Kingdom in the future only. Fight today for his Kingdom of righteousness, peace and love. *Amen.*

Sermon to My Own Soul

MY SOUL

I can no longer speak to the One who created me. I can no longer cry out to him with my voice. I can no longer speak across the distance to my brothers and sisters.

Today, for the first time, I burst out into yelling cries, for no obvious reason. I have often heard such cries, interrupting for a few moments the deep silence of our prison. We all knew then that one of us had become mad. The cries very soon ceased. I did not know how the guards quietened those whose nerves had cracked. Now I know.

They have put me in a strait-jacket, very tightly bound. They have put a gag in my mouth.

The only one to whom I can speak is you, my soul. David often spoke to his own soul, asking it to praise the Lord, or questioning why it was troubled. But David, too, knew madness. The Bible recounts how he pretended to be a lunatic while living with the Philistines. Psychiatrists tell us that nobody simulates madness unless he has a tendency towards it. I will do what David did. I will now deliver, in utter silence, a sermon to you, my soul.

I ask you, first of all, to take knowledge of yourself and to declare, like God, "I am."

The body needs few things in order to be fully satisfied: simple food, warmth, exercise, rest and a partner of the opposite sex. My body had all these things, but, notwithstanding, I was not happy; I sighed for something more. Who was this "I", dissatisfied when the body had plenty of all that it needed? It was you, my soul.

It was you who wished to know, out of purely scientific interest, about galaxies far away, and about facts of prehistory, which have absolutely no influence on my bodily state. It was you who took delight in art and philosophy, but also in exaggerations and refinements of bodily needs, even when these did harm to the body.

Don't you see, my soul, how right Jesus was in saying that "man shall not live by bread alone"?[1] I get one slice of bread every Tuesday. And what bread! But I don't just vegetate. I live. I sometimes laugh heartily at jokes which I tell myself, being alone in my cell. I think about politics, about how nations which I have never seen should be ruled; I remember works of art; I lead a life of worship. All this is you. Say, my soul, "I am."

A few days ago a Christian prisoner, unable to bear the tortures any more, and fearing that he would finally betray the brethren, jumped from the window of the third floor during an interrogation. He was healthy. He was not satisfying a need of the body by destroying himself. You know my secret. You know the place where I have hidden some thirty sleeping pills which, taken at once, will ensure that I do not become a Judas. These suicides are acts of love and honour. They protect the Underground church. Love, decency, honour, belong to you, my soul, and not to the body. I am gagged and cannot speak. But because of this, you must speak even more loudly, and assert yourself: "I am."

You saw me dancing when I was in unspeakable pain. You saw me dancing with heavy chains around my ankles. Who was the one who exuberantly rejoiced? It was not my body. My body had no reason to dance. There was no music to incite it to do so. It was you, my soul.

Take knowledge of yourself, my soul, and take knowledge of your incomparable value. The body will die. Around me, prisoners are dying, because of the great hunger, the cold and the tortures. But who has ever seen a soul die? I have lost everything I had in the world, but if you are saved, I shall have kept the pearl of greatest price.

The enemies of Jesus took away everything he had. Naked,

he hung on a cross. His foes stood around it, rejoicing. But at the last minute he spoiled their joy by saying: "Father, into thy hands I surrender my spirit." He had one thing which they could not take from him. And by this he lives and rules for ever more.

There is no one who can destroy you, my soul.

You must only repent, in the biblical sense of the word. The Greek word "*metanoia*" has nothing to do with remorse about sin, with which we confuse repentance in our modern languages. Etymologically, *metanoia* means "a change of mind" or "to go beyond reason". Parallel biblical expressions are "to receive a new heart", "to become a new creature", "to deny oneself", "to be born again", "to become a child", "to be clean every whit".

I will tell you what is wrong with you, my soul; why you need a radical transformation.

Some believe that when we repent we have to change the content of our soul. They fill their souls with heavenly thoughts and feelings instead of earthly ones. But can a damaged car be repaired by changing the passengers who travel in it? The experience of men who deceive themselves about being Christians shows that a broken car does not move, no matter who are the passengers. You may have all your thoughts and feelings directed towards God, and still not be in friendship with him, because the intimate structure of the soul, its psychological mechanism, its fundamental defect, has not been corrected. Repentance must affect not only our thoughts and feelings and wills but the very being of the soul, its complicated organism out of which thoughts, emotions and actions flow.

My soul, I reproach you for one great defect: the lack of a sense of proportion.

Jesus tried to convey this sense in the words "Fools and blind . . . whether is *greater* . . . ? Ye have omitted the *weightier* matters of the law . . ."[2] St. Paul asks: "Are we *stronger* than the Lord?"[3]

We have to distinguish what is smaller, less important, weaker, from what is greater, weightier, stronger.

You, my soul, have made yourself the pivot round which everything else has to revolve. The animals cannot speak, as I cannot because of being gagged. They have interesting things to say. The story of Balaam's ass shows this. How much our dog could have told us! He knew beforehand that I was going to be arrested. He was miserable for two weeks, and barked the whole time. But animals cannot speak. You never used to be worried about the dumbness of animals. You are only worried now that I am gagged. But the whole Communist camp is gagged. Nobody is allowed to say everything he thinks. I am in a strait-jacket. But some angels are in everlasting chains. How much worse it must be for winged beings, accustomed to fly from planet to planet! I am obsessed only with the suffering of one little insignificant being – me. Why can't you have a right sense of proportion? Why don't you worry about yourself in proportion to the share of your suffering in the universal pain, and in proportion to what you, an unimportant man, mean in this infinite and eternal universe?

You judge things, events and men according to their usefulness or harm for *you*, as if the universe existed for you, and not the reverse.

True repentance is a reversal of proportions. God is at the centre. I am an extremely valuable being, but one of innumerable billions of beings, of whom every one has to bear the fate assigned to him by the Creator.

The soul which has repented does not become lost in details. The whole world, and not only the world of men, is passing through a huge and long-lasting catastrophe, and I am worrying about what is happening to *me*. During the war, a quarrel broke out in a family, in my presence, because the husband reproached the wife for not dusting a cupboard. At the same moment, tens of thousands of young lives were being wiped out in Stalingrad, London, France and our own country.

If this defect, this lack of a sense of proportion, is not repaired in a soul, the fact that a man has changed from being an atheist to being religious does not help him. The soul will continue to be busy with trifles, with this difference, that now they will be religious trifles. The object at which you look with short-sighted eyes will be a different object, but your eyes will remain short-sighted.

Consider yourself, my soul, as a small detail in a huge mechanism, as one cell in a vast organism. White blood corpuscles are sacrificed in order that the whole body may live and be healthy. You have to suffer for some hidden purpose of God, about which you know as little as the white corpuscle knows why it has to die.

Let it be enough for you that you are suffering for the Kingdom of God.[4] All suffering serves this final cause.

Jesus looked on his suffering like this. He accepted it willingly and, even on the cross, thought not about himself but about the thief near him, about his mother and about you. Drown your small suffering in the vast ocean of pain. Believe that there is meaning in it, and you will be comforted.

Listen to me, my soul, and praise the Lord in all his doings. *Amen.*

Word Made Flesh

DEAR BROTHERS AND SISTERS

In Hebrew, *"davar"* is a homonym which means both "word" and "thing"; the real thing. In the language of the chosen people, words are not only symbols and echoes of a reality but they are themselves reality.

When St. John thought out in Hebrew the prologue of his Gospel, he meant it to mean: "In the beginning was the reality. And the reality was with God. And the reality was God."

I almost never sleep at night. There is a blessing in night vigils. "Behold, now bless ye the Lord, all ye servants of the Lord, which *by night* stand in the house of the Lord."[1] During the night men meet to practise evil. Burglaries, murders and rapes occur at night. Stalin did not sleep during the night. That is when he received people and planned his mass murders. Saints must use the weapon of night vigils to counteract the power of darkness. Those who have to work during the day cannot do this. But I have the privilege of being an isolated prisoner. I can sleep during the day. I can keep vigil during the night.

I pass my nights in spiritual exercises, in prayer, in travelling in spirit round the world and remembering every country before God, in preparing and delivering sermons.

Every night I also compose a poem. I compose it in my mind, not having any paper to write it down.

Poor poems of an ungifted spirit! What are they compared to the works of the great artists? But even so, in my concern with metre and rhyme, I can feel the difficulty which poets must have in putting love and wisdom and life into poetry.

The words, confined in verses, feel as I felt when I was put in a strait-jacket.

The Word became flesh two thousand years ago. The Word would like to be flesh today, too, and not merely a piece of poetry. The Word desires to be incarnate once more in a man who can perform deeds of love, and can also speak harshly for righteousness' sake and rebuke wrongdoing, as Jesus did – a man who leaves all, loves all and offers himself as a sacrifice for all, even for those who betray him and scourge him; even for those whom he himself has had to strike with a whip for the sake of justice.

The word of God and the spirit of love are always longing for incarnation. Christ was incarnate not only in the carpenter Jesus; he also lived in St. Paul. We throw only words into the agitated sea of this world, and the multitude of words takes the place of reality.

God has brought me into the sphere of silence. The silence around me is absolute. You cannot hear the guards approach. God wishes me to unlearn words. It is becoming more and more difficult for me to formulate long, clear sentences. Perhaps they are putting some drug in the food to destroy my mind.

I live in profound silence, a silence like that inhabited by the fish in the depths of the sea. The secret sign of the first Christians was a fish.

I am beginning to love this silence. I sometimes make up verses to pass the time, but what I would really like would be to make men, each one of whom would be a fine piece of poetry. In the original Greek of Ephesians, it is written that Christians are the poem (*poema*) of God.[2] So God is a poet, too. His poems are serene, flexible, rich in meaning. He has embodied his poems in flesh. Each one has a different subject. One is the embodiment of heroism, another of sanctity, another of wisdom, yet another of practical common sense. Christians are not only different, but also sometimes divergent and even contradictory characters. But every one is pleasing to the Lord.

According to Ephesians[3] the role of the pastor is not to make sermons but to make saints.

I would also like such a task. First of all, I would like to make myself into a temple of embodied love, so that those who follow the wise men and shepherds of old may see in me Christ in miniature, and worship the Saviour in me.

Instead of a world in which bookshops sell volumes of sermons and poetry, I would like a world in which each man and woman is a poem of high thought, filled with melody and colour.

If I am a hindrance to the coming of such a world, may God kill me here in prison! But this is how the world should be.

I will do my part towards the coming of such a kingdom by following the example of Laban. His name in Hebrew means "white". He had two daughters, Rachel and Leah. A young man, Jacob, loved the beautiful Rachel. But Laban did not allow him to have her, unless he took the ugly Leah too. Laban was a just man, and did not allow preferential love. Christian love must embrace both the good and the bad.

Goethe called colour the suffering of light, because colour is the result of the tearing asunder of light beams while passing through a prism. Full, undivided light is white, *"laban"*. White embraces everybody and everything you see, and even more. So the man who cultivates the white in his soul walks with devotion, as in a liturgy, through the world of the unloved and unlovely Leahs, whose constantly weeping eyes are unpleasant to look upon. It is a world full of girls whose hearts are broken because nobody loves them. Not being loved, they become uglier and uglier, and even a saint like Jacob does not want them. He desires only to pass his life with the beautiful Rachel. For her he works zealously for fourteen years, and it seems to him but a few days. He would not have worked one day for Leah.

Within the *ecclesia*, the church, there is an *ecclesiola*, a little church, which accepts the good and the bad, which embraces both the beautiful and the ugly. If God has united in the same church a criminal like a Borgia and a saint like Francis of

Assisi, and brought into the same institution the priests who betrayed us and the martyrs who suffer with me, then I, too, must love them all.

Jesus showed his love first for the ugly Leahs by sitting at table with publicans and sinners to bring them to repentance. There are beautiful Rachels near me in prison who do not feel his presence. They will receive their part, only much later.

Love all men, my dear brothers, but bestow the greatest part of your love on the ugliest souls. They need your love more than anyone else. You, my fellow-prisoners, must show your greatest love to the Communist torturers and those who betrayed us. The beautiful souls can endure without tokens of your love. Spend your energy where it is most needed!

I lay especially on your hearts love towards the pastors and priests who collaborate with the Communist persecutors and denounce their brethren. I am afraid at the thought that things may develop in our country towards the situation that exists in the Soviet Union, where in many instances these traitors have been lynched or stabbed by Christians of the Underground church. The church of the catacombs has to be protected from traitors, and if there is no other way, they resort to such means. The church of the first centuries did it, too, though those who teach church history don't say very much about it.

But this is the extreme solution. In the Nazi times, we won for Christ men who had betrayed us and put us in prison. We should do our utmost to achieve this now, too. Let the word become flesh in us, flesh of a man who accepts the kiss of Judas and calls him friend, even when he comes at the head of an armed gang to arrest you. *Amen.*

A Children's Sunday School

MOST BELOVED CHILDREN

Today the Communists beat me heavily. In the end I fainted. They revived me by pouring water on me, and then began to beat me again.

And then the worst happened. The door burst open, and into the room where I was being interrogated rushed our brothers and sisters – Brother Davidescu, the one with the long beard, and Brother Marinov, and old Auntie Ionescu, and Suzanne, and all the others whom I love so much. I wondered how they had got into the prison. Then they began to beat me, they to whom I have never done any wrong. Then the door opened again. This time it was Binzea, my wife, and Mihai, my son. They also spat on me, and mocked me, telling me that they were ashamed to have me for a husband and father. And Mihai put out his fist to strike me. It was too much. I fainted again. When I awoke I was alone with the interrogators. The whole scene had been a hallucination.

I knew then that I had gone mad, as so many have done before me, whose yelling cries I can hear resounding in the arched corridor.

And now you have come, my dear children, to fill my lonely cell. You really are here. I don't know if it is what those who are sane call the real "here", or if it is my "here", the here of a lunatic. But you are here. And it is not only you, children, who fill my Sunday-school class. This time I can see your guardian angels, too, hoping that I will tell you the right thing, thirsty to listen themselves to some beautiful story about Jesus.

And look, there he is himself, the holy child. In the old days, he appeared in the shape of a child to St. Jerome, the monk who first translated the Bible into Latin.

Jerome was working on his translation in Bethlehem, the birthplace of our Lord. As he prayed, Jesus appeared to him in the shape of a child. This filled the heart of the saint with such overwhelming sweetness that he said: "Beloved Jesus, I would like with all my heart to give you a present. Tell me, what would please you most?" The child smiled, and answered: "Heaven and earth and all that is in them are mine. What can you give me?" The saint said again: "But I love you, and wish to make you a gift. Will you accept all the little money which I, a monk, possess?" The child replied again, still smiling: "Give your money to the poor. I have no use for it." St. Jerome insisted: "I cannot let you go away empty-handed. What shall I give you?" Then the child became very grave and said: "If you wish to bring me an offering which will fill my heart with joy, give me all your sins and all your lusts. I will die because of them on the cross. There is no other gift which would fill my heart with such gladness as this."

Blessed is he that cometh in the Name of the Lord! Here, among us, is the child Jesus. Let us bring him this gift – our untruthfulness, our selfishness, our anger, our bitterness. And so he will have passed his time with us in joy.

St. Anthony of Padua, when he was still a child, also met Jesus. There was a knock at the gate of his home, and Anthony ran to see who was there. Opening the gate, he saw a beggar in rags, shivering in the frost of a winter day. Taking pity on him, Anthony said: "I will ask my father to give you some warm clothes." The beggar answered: "It is very cold in your world, but I am not begging for clothes." The child then said: "You must be hungry. Come in, and my mother will give you some food." The beggar replied: "I am hungry, but I do not beg for bread." Astonished, Anthony asked: "Why then did you knock at our gate?" The beggar said: "I have come to ask you to give me your heart." The child stepped backward: "But if I give you my heart, I will die." Then the beggar opened a bag which he carried on his shoulder, and took out from it some hearts, saying: "This is the heart of St. Paul, and this of Mary Madgalene, and this of St. Ignatius. All those who have given their hearts to me, far from dying, are alive eternally," Then Anthony understood that the one who stood before him was Jesus himself, and he became his follower.

Let us also give him our hearts.

And now I will tell him, and you, and your guardian angels, a story about him.

Jesus's earthly father, Joseph, was poor. He could not afford to give him a proper education. When the child reached the age of twelve, he told him: "Now you must make an end of playing and dreaming. I will make you into a carpenter, like me."

The next day he went with the child into the forest to cut trees. But this time he could not touch the trees with his axe. Again and again he was stopped by the child, who said: "Father, you know that the Scriptures forbid killing. This tree is young and has not yet lived its life. Let it continue to enjoy the sun. See how, seeking the light, it has lifted itself towards the heights. There will be men enough ready to kill it when it has lived one year longer . . . And do not cut that one. See how many ants there are at its foot. How busily they gather herbs and little pieces of straw! I am afraid that, if you cut down the tree, many of them will be killed . . . And save that one. It has a nest of birds in its branches. Their chirping is heard in heaven. The baby birds will die, and you will be accused in the country beyond the stars of their murder . . . And leave this one, because the sound of the saw, as its teeth enter the wood, will go up to heaven, to the Father who has commanded us to have mercy on men and trees, on animals and birds, on flowers and plants. Holy eyes are weeping at the sorrow of them all."

Jesus pleaded so fervently, and so many tears ran down his cheeks, that Joseph sat down in the shade to comfort him. It was the second Sabbath that week. A leaf whispered to another: "It is the Saviour." Ants played around their feet. The birds sang: "Our longing is fulfilled." There was no cloud in the sky.

The child laid his head in Joseph's lap. Joseph played with the child's curls. The son was the teacher, the father the disciple. The angels watched them both.

The child asked: "Tell me, Father, why do you have an axe? You know that iron tools were invented by a descendant of the wicked Cain. When the Romans asked you to make a cross on which to crucify a man, you also shortened the life of a tree. I have seen men carrying their crosses to the place of execution. I have seen them falling under the burden. You have told me that this will be my end, too. Will a tree lose its life for me, before I lose mine for mankind? I cry when I see men cutting rods, because rods are used for beating children. You cut something which has life, in order to use it to commit brutalities."

As the oil runs down the beard of a priest when he is anointed, so the tears ran down Joseph's beard, a sign that the words had touched his heart.

But he tried to make excuses: "If a carpenter takes pity on the trees, he will starve." He spoke too soon. The idea of death as a result of doing right fell on fertile soil.

The child said: "If by not killing trees for carpentry, we die of hunger, we will go to the country where there is no more death, and where we will love each other all day long. There, Mother will weep no more. You know that here men mock her. She will sit at my right hand, you at my left, and I, in the middle, will love you. I shall not become a carpenter, but I will be the one who dies that the trees may have life abundantly, and that there may be one more sun in the sky. I will not destroy the life of the trees."

On that day the trees remained alive. The child was their saviour. For the dark forest, he foreshadowed a cloudless day.

But Joseph the poor carpenter had great burdens. There was a whole family to be cared for. He was not a child who could afford to lead a life of dreams.

The next day he took Jesus into the carpenter's shop. He taught him to measure a board with a yard-stick, to draw a

straight line on it, to use a plane and the different tools. In this
life you have to work. Otherwise you die.

But Mary his mother noticed that every day the child became
more pale and serious. He was silent, and kept hidden from
everybody the reason for his pallor. It was because, as often as
the hammer hit the wood, he felt the blows in his own body.
He wept every time the saw bit into the wood. He fell prostrate
to the floor, his tears running down on to the sawdust which
was sacrificed to provide beds and chairs on which men could
rest; in the same way he himself would one day be sacrificed
that others might have eternal rest. He wept because he had
made his decision. He would atone for the sins committed by
men against the trees. On a tree which had been the victim of
injustice, he would be the sacrifice.

And now every little branch can wait patiently in silence.
Jesus died on the tree to give assurance that you, broken
branches, will be grafted again into the olive tree. Jesus fought
your battle on the wood of the tree, to prepare for you a won-
derful future.

So the child Jesus fulfilled his apprenticeship. He learned
to be a carpenter, a carpenter who practised his art weeping, the
carpenter who made the gates to heaven.

You, the one who created me – I do not address you by the
name men usually call you. I remember that St. Paphnutius,
when he had brought to Christ the renowned courtesan Thais,
told her: "Your lips are not worthy to pronounce the holy
name of the Creator. Your prayer should only be, 'You who
have made me, have mercy on me.'" She prayed like this for
three years, alone in her nun's cell. After three years, a brother
had a vision of a beautiful soul on a bed covered with roses,
waited on by angels. He was sure that this must be the place
reserved in heaven for St. Anthony the Great, the founder of
monasticism. But Anthony told him that he had seen the place
of Thais, the humble sinner who had refrained from pro-
nouncing your name.

You, the one who created me – The children whose presence
I enjoyed so much have vanished. So also have their guardian

angels and the holy child. So this was a hállucination, too, like the one I had this morning when they beat me. I really have become mad.

I have visited many mental asylums. Some of the patients are happy. They believe themselves to be emperors or saints. Others suffer from continual nightmares, believing that they are persecuted, in danger and being tortured.

Would it be too much to ask you just one thing? Give me a happy madness. Let me see the children thronging round me, and let me see their beautiful angels. Let me always behold the child Jesus. It may be that there are some who would not even consider this a hallucination, but as a vision from you. These, perhaps, would be mad like me. But they will appreciate what I tell them, and I will be comforted.

This much, a happy madness, I ask from you. *Amen.*

Gagged Again

DEAR SOUL OF MINE

I will speak with you again today. Again there have been the yelling cries, which neither I nor the other prisoners can master. I am in a strait-jacket and gagged for the second time. With whom else could I speak now but you?

I wonder how St. Francis of Assisi would have felt in my place.

I remember his conversation with Brother Leo, who asked him wherein is perfect joy. Does it lie in knowing many things? Francis denied this. Leo asked again if perfect joy lies in being a prophet and knowing the mysteries of God. Francis shook his head silently to show that the brother had missed the point. Leo asked again if the winning of many souls for Christ would not be perfect joy. The answer was still the same: "No." Leo inquired whether great sanctity, enabling one even to perform miracles for the good of men, would not be perfect joy.

Francis answered: "None of these things can give perfect joy. We shall know such joy only if, when we reach St. Mary of the Angels, soaked with rain, hungry and shivering with cold, the doorkeeper drives us out, mocking us with cruel words as beggars and rogues. We shall know perfect joy if we remain hungry outside the walls of the monastery, enduring the rain and the mud, and if we endure this with gladness and patience and thankfulness. The cross is the only tree on which the flower of perfect joy will grow."

I have the cross. So I decided to be joyful, and I danced. I spun round until my mind became completely blank. My whole body was in a sweat when I fell on to my bed with tears running down my cheeks, while the guards, who had been looking through the peep-hole in the door, laughed.

Now I am living my life backwards, from the eternal bliss which waits for all who love the Lord, through the moment when you, my soul, will be released from the prison of the body, to my present state. Then I remember how a few minutes ago I could still move my arms. I remember the beautiful years with my church and my family, and then my whole life backwards until my early childhood. I can somehow remember being a babe in arms. Before that I was an embryo, watched over by a guardian angel. Before that I was in the loins of my forefathers. I know so many of them, having had the privilege of being Jewish. I know that Abraham was my ancestor, and Terah and the others. I was in Adam falling into sin, and before that enjoying fellowship with God. And before that? I was a spirit with God. Before that . . . there was no me and he. There was only the One in full serenity from all eternity.

Why, my soul, are you so stupidly concerned with the latest event, the fact that I have been put into a strait-jacket and gagged?

Uninitiated souls always judge by the latest impression. A wrong word spoken by somebody today makes us forget the many good deeds we have observed in the same person over many years. One kind gesture makes us trust a man whose past record does not make him trustworthy. Uninitiated men are incapable of taking into account all they know about a man before judging him. For them, only the latest event counts.

The Pharisees judged like this. For them, Jesus was a sinner, because he broke the Sabbath. That was all they could think of. All the good works and teachings of Jesus were forgotten. Can I form a right opinion of a man, having in view only his breaking of the law in one particular instance, and losing sight of his total personality?

There are men who repent outwardly, and now live in the church instead of living in the world as before. But the mechanism of their soul has remained the same. So they now judge the brethren according to the latest event, instead of judging men of the world in this way. But their thinking has remained false. They even judge God according to this criterion; they praise him when he gives them something good, and begin to doubt when affliction comes.

But you, my soul, must not judge according to the fact that for the last hour I have been in a strait-jacket. Keep in view the whole of life and its whole orbit. There is something more than the infinite. There is the transfinite. If, starting from a certain point, I draw an endless line, its value is infinite. But if from the same point I draw two endless lines in opposite directions, that is transfinite. You are more than eternal, my soul, you are from God to God, and you will enter again into him, enriched by human experience. "God saw every thing that he had made, and, behold, it was very good."[1] Only when you see everything will you see how good it is. The most beautiful painting is only a formless mixture of colours and senseless lines until it is completed. The most beautiful sculpture is just a hewn stone until it receives its definitive shape.

Wait, my soul, until you are again at large in God. Then you will see the sense of the strait-jacket, too.

And then, being gagged again and again, perhaps I shall begin to like the gagging. It takes me out of the sphere of words, in which men are imprisoned. Preachers are specially exposed to the temptation of becoming talkers.

Words, which were first formed for naming surrounding realities, become emptied, with time, of their original meaning. Retarded souls continue to accord them the same value and respect as when they had a rich content. They don't realise that they are now merely outwardly beautiful dolls, stuffed with straw.

The word "bishop" originally meant the chief pastor, the most advanced in faith, the man who gave his life for his sheep in time of persecution. Now he is a man of some academic learning, chosen by men who often are not children of God themselves. Even before my arrest, all our Orthodox bishops, except one, had subscribed to what the Communist killers of Christians demanded. The Reformed bishop did the same. Now they praise the Communists and denounce their own sheep.

So the words "priest", "pastor", "rabbi", "church", "Christain", "Jew", "believer", "faith", "religion", "art", have entirely changed their meaning.

The fact that I am now gagged gives me freedom to see the reality which corresponds to a word today.

The Communists are torturing us in the beautiful name of a happy future for mankind.

"Let every man be . . . slow to speak",[2] which means that he should always consider whether every word has a corresponding reality. My chief interrogator is called Dulgheru, which means Carpenter. But this is only a name. He never held a plane in his hands.

One of the high priests who judged Jesus had the name of Annas, which means "pity".

Bless, my soul, the Communists who, by gagging me, free me from the vanity of words, and give me an insight into reality. There is a meaning in this gagging, too. Thanks be to God. *Amen.*

Visible Wounds

DEAR BROTHERS AND SISTERS

For a few days I could not preach to you as usual. The physical pain was too great. Still, there was some joy in the pain. Up to now, they have beaten and whipped me. Now, for the first time, they have tortured me, so that visible marks will remain on my body until death, or perhaps even after.

I used to wonder how it was that the resurrected body of our Lord bore the marks of wounds. Can a resurrected body look like this? Will we be resurrected with rheumatism, deformities, twisted limbs? Will the resurrected body bear the marks of the experiences through which it has passed? Jesus spoke about some who will enter into life having one eye or one hand.[1]

He had to be resurrected with marks on his body, in order that, as often as the sins of men are brought before the Father, he may show his wounds, received in order that the sinner may be saved.

By this sacrifice of his, I am saved, too.

But perhaps my scars also will be helpful. My prayers for my torturers will perhaps be more effective if I can show the Father the wounds I received from them. If *I* can continue to love them, if *I* can forgive, why should God exclude them from his love and not forgive them?

And then, perhaps, perhaps there is a slight possibility that I shall one day be out of prison and in the West. Then I shall be able to show the unbelieving Thomases, who do not accept that Communism is crime on a huge scale under the cloak of an ideal, what Jesus showed to his doubting apostle and so convinced him – the marks of the wounds.

There is a blessing in the tortures through which I have passed. We must thank God for everything. While they tortured me, I could not think. Just one word flashed through my mind once: "We were appointed thereunto"[2] – that is, to afflictions.

The tortures have made some transformations in my soul. They have lessened my desire to go to heaven. What happiness would it be for me to sit in bliss in heaven, knowing that others are being tortured in the meantime on earth? I would be among the few of whom Jesus spoke who are ready to leave Abraham's bosom and be with the tormented souls in order to comfort them.[3] My wish is rather that God's will should be done on earth as it is in heaven. Why not make a heaven out of earth, as Jesus taught us to pray?

I long for an earth filled with righteousness and justice and love; a world where even the animals would live in paradise, lions lying down with lambs and not devouring them.

When I was in prison under the Nazis we noticed how the birds seemed to have a sympathy for humans, and how they always had a presentiment of what would happen to us. There were pigeons in the prison yard. They used to come to our barred windows, and we gave them crumbs of bread. It was not just one man's imagination, all the prisoners agreed that they observed, before days of heavy beatings, that the pigeons would beat their wings and flutter frantically, uttering cries of alarm. The farmers with whom I am imprisoned tell me, in our long conversations in code, that their dogs knew beforehand about their arrests, and could not be stopped from howling all night long, as they had never done before.

In my cell there is only one animal, a spider. I don't know how he happened to enter the underground cell. But one day he was there. He just took advantage of a moment when the guard unlocked the door. He made his web. We became good friends. I fed him. I talked to him. I had observed that he was unusually agitated the day before I was taken out for torture. It may have been a coincidence. I don't know. But I have the feeling that he sympathises with me. We ought even more to sympathise with the animal world, and wish for them and for ourselves, not that we should go to the Kingdom of God – the way might be too far for a spider – it would be much simpler if his Kingdom were to come here. Jesus taught us to pray for this. Then criminals and lions and foxes would have a much easier entrance.

On that day the world from which we come will seem like the place where we were caterpillars. In the sufferings of today, we are cocoons. One day we shall be butterflies. We shall be able to fly from star to star, not neglecting our own planet. The angels were ascending and descending between earth and heaven on Jacob's ladder. So there is a ladder uniting earth to God. Sometimes we will ascend. Then we will descend again. There will be no difference, because it will be on earth as it is in heaven. Those who are Christ's will then be like Christ. To be with them will be like being with the Son of God himself.

I am much more concerned now with making earth a paradise than with going to a heavenly paradise. This means a fight in every sphere of life to defeat the red dragon and all the other manifestations of the apocalyptic beast.[4]

Dear brothers and sisters, I want you to fight for the triumph of righteousness and love, that is for the triumph of Christ on earth; but remember that it is always easier to fight for a principle than to live up to it. Don't choose the easy way, but the way of the Cross. Don't remain yourselves unrighteous and lacking in sweetness while you are fighting for righteousness. Clothe yourselves with Christ and with all his virtues, and so fight.

It is not only I who sit in prison. You are all in the prisons of your sinful selves, and of your wrong and limited ideas. Let Jesus free you of these! Then you will be able to fight and to attain your aim.

I am so happy to have been able to speak with you again tonight, after a short pause.

As I told you, I had some small, flickering joy in those days too, thinking about the value of the torture marks. But don't think that I am a hero, and that I just whistled and laughed when I was in great pain. It was rather a time of great depression. I could not pray. I could not realise the presence of God, except in very short glimpses, which lasted perhaps only seconds.

The marks are a blessing. The time of depression has been a blessing, too. It showed me how horrible eternity without God would be. Those days without feeling him near were each a thousand years long. I realised how horrible it would be to remain in hell with unrepentant criminals who through eternity would swear, curse and think only evil, as my Communist torturers do. God brought me into a Communist prison, God made me pass through tortures, and through the dark night of the soul, in order that I may learn what hell is and do my utmost to avoid it.

My brothers, strive after heaven, a heaven which will comprehend the earth too.

There is a legend which says that a monk once left his monastery to cut trees in a wood. In the forest a bird from paradise was singing. He listened to her beautiful trills for a while, then he quickly finished his work and returned to the monastery. But the porter was not the usual one. He would not even allow him to enter. He gave his name. It was completely unknown. He asked for the abbot. A man came whom he had never seen before. It was in vain that he protested that he had left the monastery only an hour ago. Nobody recognised him. Finally, somebody remembered that the monastery kept a story about a monk who had left the monastery centuries ago to cut wood and had disappeared without leaving any trace. The heavenly song of a bird from paradise, which seemed to have lasted only a few minutes, had lasted for centuries counting after the human manner.

The days during which you have not heard from me have been days of depression, but a depression filled with deep meaning. There have been rare moments of joy, when I realised the value of the wounds I have received. But I finally came out of my depression because I too heard a song from paradise. I have heard in my lifetime the music of Beethoven and Bach, but how poor they are in comparison with the song I have now heard!

Brothers and sisters, fight to fill the earth with this heavenly song! Forsake all the old songs for this one: "*Shiru le-Adonai shir hadash*" – "Sing unto the Lord a new song." This is the commandment given to the angels. Just listen. You will learn it from them. *Amen.*

Binzea

DEAR BROTHERS AND SISTERS

Today the subject of my sermon will be Sabina, my wife, whom you and I love. We all call her Binzea.

If Ruth and Esther can be the subjects of whole books of the Bible, why should not the wife of a preacher be the subject of his sermon? Binzea is dear to God, and dear to me as Ruth was to Boaz and Esther to Ahasuerus.

Today I saw myself in a mirror, the first time for two years. They had to make repairs to our latrines, so the guards took us to theirs, and there was a mirror.

A homeric laughter overcame me, looking at myself. I used to be considered a handsome man. Now I am thin, ugly, with black circles under my eyes. So that is what remains of bodily beauty! And one day I shall be even uglier than that. I shall be a skeleton with a skull.

Coming back to my cell, I remembered another time when I had stood in front of a mirror. I had often thought about the words "God created man in his own image, in the image of God created he him", and I had wondered in what our Godlikeness consists. I could not find a satisfactory answer. One day I stood before a mirror, asking myself once again the question: "Which feature of mine corresponds to a feature of God?" My wife, having an intuition of what was going through my mind, silently came and stood beside me. And then I understood at once. "God created man in his own image . . . male and female created he them."[1]

Our Godlikeness consists in the union of the two sexes. Through this we become "pro-creators", or deputy creators.

We become capable of creating eternal beings, just as God created Adam and Eve.

The unmarried also have a partner of the opposite sex in the spiritual realm, the girls their animus, the men their anima, as Jung calls them – their ideal love, whom they have never met and with whom they could never unite. But life is infinite. They will unite.

Binzea is the one who, by union with me, made me become more Godlike. Although I was converted before she was, it is to her that I owe my being a Christian today.

I remember the prison days with her in the Nazi time. Then we met every day in the corridor and could take walks together. I remember how, on another occasion when I was arrested, she demanded that she should go to prison with me.

Then the Communists came to power. A high Orthodox prelate, stooge of the Communists but personally friendly to me, had warned me that the decision had been made to arrest me. I had an opportunity to flee. Should I use it or not?

When I consulted my wife, she answered: "If you flee, how will you ever be able to preach again from the text, 'The good shepherd giveth his life for the sheep. But he that is an hireling, and not the shepherd, whose own the sheep are not, seeth the wolf coming and leaveth the sheep and fleeth . . .'?" [2]

I was still tempted to flee. Then one day I was visited by a pastor for whose conversion God had used me. He had been an alcoholic. I found him drunk on the street, refusing to go home. So I accompanied him from bar to bar, and spoke to him. When he awoke from his drunkenness next day, he was a new man. And now he reminded me of this. During our conversation, he repeated again and again: "What struck me most in what you told me then was the verse: 'Escape for thy life, look not behind thee.' " [3]

When he left, I asked my wife: "Were not his continual repetitions a guidance from God that I must save my life by fleeing?" She answered: "Yes, you must save your life. But whoever saves his life in this world, will lose it. The man who loses his life will save it."

So I decided to stay. I don't regret it.

I do regret that I was kidnapped from the street by the Communist police. If they had taken me from my home, I would have been able to ask her forgiveness for having often been mean to her.

Now I sometimes surprise myself by saying, instead of "Jesus, help me!", "Binzea, help me!" She is so like Jesus. Those who followed St. Paul followed Jesus. For sick men, it was the same thing to appeal to Jesus himself or to his apostles for help. They were cured just the same. One day Christians will be like Christ. To talk with them will be like talking with the Saviour. It may not even be wrong to say, "Binzea, help me." It would be considered quite normal if she were near me. But now, in my narrow cell, I am free from the limitations of space. There is no near and far. Why should I not appeal to her? All good men of all ages are close to each other and can help one another. It is probably from this experience of Christians in great suffering in the first centuries that the practice of appealing to the saints arose, with all that remained valuable or became harmful in it in later years.

Binzea did not know what it was to avoid danger. She incited me to speak out openly against the Communists at the Congress of Cults convened by them in our Parliament building.

I once quoted to her a Cambodian proverb: "When two elephants are fighting, the ant should step aside." She laughed and said: "I am not a Cambodian, I am a Rumanian. We have a proverb of our own: 'A little log can overturn a large cart.' "

Where is she likely to be now? Probably in a prison cell somewhere near me. I heard a woman shrieking. I could have sworn that it was her voice. I last saw her in the spirit. She was bleeding, as if she had been heavily tortured.

While I wept with longing for her, the thought occurred to me: It is written that "the blood of Jesus Christ, his Son, cleanseth us from all sin".[4] But where is the blood of Jesus? Where can I find it to make it cleanse my sins? The glorified body of

Jesus had no blood. The Lord used, instead of the standard Jewish expression "flesh and blood" (*basar vedam*), the words "flesh and bones".[5] The blood which he spilled from the scourging, the crown of thorns, the crucifixion, no longer exists, just as the blood of all those who have died has passed, over the centuries, through the thousands of transformations of nature and does not exist anywhere.

Then where is the blood of Christ which can save me from sin? I am afraid the blood of Jesus about which certain priests and pastors preach is more like the artificial blood used in cinema studios in scenes of violence, which consists only of chemicals painted on the actor's face.

The name of Christ can be used in two senses. It can mean both the historical person of two thousand years ago, and the mystical body of which the glorified Jesus is the head and we are all the body.[6] This Christ bleeds continually. There has never been a day in history when at least one member of this mystical body has not bled. Their blood is the blood of Christ. Everything in them belongs to Christ. And they fill up in their flesh that which is behind of the afflictions of Christ.[7] They perpetuate the sacrifice, and so it is his blood which continually cleanses.

We apply to events a false notion of time. When we travel in a train we have the impression that the villages and towns are passing us. We say that one station has passed and another follows. The truth is that all towns coexist at the same time. What we see is a delusion of our senses. So our mind, limited in time, sees some events of history as belonging to the past, and others as future. The reality is that there exists only an eternal "now", in which the bleeding of Jesus on Calvary is as actual today as it was two thousand years ago. And the bleeding of martyrs from before the time of Jesus and those of all centuries all belong to the eternal now.

In the vast picture of this eternal now, there is also a spot where I will see Binzea again, and you will see your loved ones, in eternal gladness. Good night, Binzea. God give you peace.

Brothers and sisters, let us love our wives and husbands as Christ loved us and gave himself for us!

"If the salt have lost his savour, wherewith shall it be salted?" [8] Salt is sodium chloride. The salt molecule can lose one of its atoms. It then ceases to be salt, and loses its savour. It can become salt again so long as it remains open to receive union with another atom. No man is lost as long as he has somebody to give him instruction which will "salt" him. Now, when the best of your teachers sit in jail, and you have so many unreliable ones who have compromised with Communism, the one who can salt you best might be your wife or husband. Profit from this possibility for as long as you are together. *Amen.*

The Victims of My Life

So here you are again, the victims of my life. Good evening! I know nothing which cleanses the soul so well as a straight face-to-face discussion with you.

I believe that truth is to be found not only in the Bible. I believe that I can rely on a book of arithmetic in its own sphere as much as on the Bible. I also believe in Shakespeare. As the Scriptures teach you the maximum which a man can know about God, so Shakespeare teaches you the most a man can know about human character. *Romeo and Juliet* can even be seen as an allegory of the love between the Saviour and his bride, just as we find an allegory in the *Song of Solomon*, and the Hindus in the *Bhagavad Gita*.

There are only two things I wonder about Shakespeare. First, why does he not describe Christian characters? Secondly, I wonder whether the apparition of the ghost of Hamlet's father, and the presence of the murdered Banquo at Macbeth's table, represent fiction or reality. I have always been rather inclined to consider them as a description of reality.

In the Nazi prison I was with a murderer who denied his crime. The prosecutor put him in a solitary cell whose walls were covered with dozens of pictures of the victim. The killer pounded on the door of his cell, confessing everything and demanding only that the pictures should be removed. What was for us only a picture evoked for him a reality which was with him in the cell.

Now I am passing through the same experience. Night after night, you come. But I don't bang on the door. I do not wish to escape from your reproaches. Do not try to terrify me by

circling round me in this mad dance and pointing at me with your skeleton fingers.

I know how to dance, too. And you know that my dance is more effective than yours, just as the miracles of Moses were greater than those of the Egyptian magicians who opposed him.

You dance? I will dance, too, singing the song which Jesus sang when he danced. Ha, ha, ha. You don't even know that he danced? Listen to the words of incantation while I dance – words which I learned from him:

"*Glory be to thee, Father. Amen.*
. . . Glory be to thee, Grace. Amen.
Glory be to thee, Spirit: Glory be to thee, Holy One:
Glory be to thy glory. Amen . . .
I would eat, and I would be eaten. Amen.
I would hear, and I would be heard. Amen . . .
Grace danceth. I would pipe; dance ye all. Amen . . .
The number Eight singeth praise with us. Amen
The number Twelve danceth on high. Amen.
The Whole on high hath part in our dancing. Amen.
Whoso danceth not, knoweth not what cometh to pass.
    Amen . . .
I would flee, and I would stay. Amen . . .
A place I have not, and I have places. Amen.
A temple I have not, and I have temples. Amen.
A lamp am I to thee that beholdest me. Amen.
A mirror am I to thee that perceivest me. Amen.
A door am I to thee that knockest at me. Amen.
A way am I to thee a wayfarer. Amen . . .
Now answer thou unto my dancing (if you can. Why can't you? Ha, ha, ha, I laugh at you!)
. . . If thou hadst known how to suffer, thou wouldest have been able not to suffer.
Learn thou to suffer, and thou shalt be able not to suffer."[1]

Why do you shrink back into a corner? Come, I have no wish to scare you. I love you all. Come on, let us reason with each other.

Yes, I killed many of you. Some of you I killed while you were yet unborn. You would have hindered my selfish life. I did not allow you to be born. Now I understand the gynaecologist who asked me to baptise him because he was haunted during the night by the many children he had killed.

You have learned the words from the Bible: "The wages of sin is death,"[2] and you threaten me with them. You may know the Bible. The devil knows it, too. But I would not call him a theologian. Neither are you. Things are not as simple as that. "Whosoever killeth shall be in danger of the judgment."[3] Have you heard? The killer is not lost. He is only in danger. He will be judged, which does not mean that he will be sentenced. He may be acquitted, too. I may explain to the Judge my bad heredity, or perhaps he will reveal it to me. I may explain to him my wrong education, my bad environment, my madness. He will know how many devils were unchained to fight against me. Weighing all this, I may still be acquitted.

And you, with whom I have committed adultery – are you not as guilty as I? Why do you throw stones at me? Or you, the holy ones who never sinned in this respect because you were impotent, or ugly or never had occasion for it. "Whosoever looks on a woman to lust after her has committed adultery in his heart."[4] And you, women, take advantage of the special kindness of Jesus towards the female sex which kept him from speaking against women who look on a man to lust after him. Don't play the righteous with me! And don't quote Bible verses at me.

We are all the same. And the eye which must be plucked out and cast from us is only the right one, the one which judges actions after the standard of righteousness and morality, not knowing that life has its own laws, and that the law of the Spirit of life, that is the simple acknowledgement of life with its intricacies, sets you free from that other law of sin and death.

I reminded Jesus once that Luther had called Christ the greatest liar, perjurer, thief, adulterer and murderer that mankind has ever known. Not in the sense that he committed these sins, but because he appropriated them to himself. I asked

Jesus: "Do you accept this charge?" and I heard a definite reply: "Yes, everything except the adultery." I was sure then that this was not his voice. I cannot believe that he is less concerned about those who neglect their parents, or cheat their employers, or gossip, or steal, than about those who experience a love story. Portia said in *The Merchant of Venice*: "The quality of mercy is not strained." It is not difficult for Jesus to appropriate to himself our adulteries, too.

And here you are, the many thousands who have listened to my sermons and read my books. You, who are of many religions and traditions, accuse me of the gravest of sins, heresy. All other sins are trifles in comparison with this, the distortion of the Word of God. Have I been guilty of this? What is truth? I stood for a truth once. Here, I am not sure of it any more. I am battered by many storms. The see of Rome attracts me with its prestige, and I wonder how I could have been anything else than Catholic. Is Adventism the real truth? There are hundreds of texts teaching us to keep the Sabbath, and not one commandment about Sunday. I see the beauty of the Orthodox tradition, quiet and deep like the Pacific Ocean. Which is the right one? Which is heresy? What ought I to have preached? I am I, and nobody else. Perhaps Protestantism, in which everyone establishes for himself his own relationship with God, is the truth. Then I am not a heretic. Each man an Abraham in personal relationship with God – that is the end result of Protestantism. What is wrong with that?

What I knew, I preached. And I don't care about your accusations. "After the way which they call heresy, so worship I the God of my fathers," said St. Paul [5] when he was charged as you charge me.

Why are you all so angry with me? What have you lost by the fact that I sinned gravely against you? Zacchaeus stole from one man perhaps a hundred dinars, with which in any case he could not have done much. But he repented and gave back to everyone fourfold. Now the man he had cheated has four hundred dinars, enough to open a little shop. Christ is called in the Hebrew of Isaiah 53 *"asham"*, which means not only "an offering for sin", but also "a restitution". To all of you whom I have robbed of this transitory life, he will give life eternal. To all of you whom I have polluted, he will give the whiteness of purity. To all of you whom I have caused to weep, he will give a pearl for every tear. To all those to whom I have taught error, he will give the final truth.

Will no reasoning quieten you? Can nothing stop you from haunting me? I see that reasoning cannot overcome the sense of guilt. Guilt drives a man mad. Arguments cannot help a madman.

Years ago they used to burn Christians at the stake. At least they had it warm. We are shivering from cold in our cells. Nevertheless I am bathed in sweat, watching you and hearing how you yell at me.

And now you are here, too, Moses. I knew you as the first keeper of the threshold of the most holy place. You, too, tell me that I have broken the law, and that therefore I am defiled and cannot enter.

You talked like this to Luther, I guess. Sometimes his hatred exploded against Jews and Catholics; at times he was as unbridled as a madman. He was one of those he called "martyrs of Providence", a man who loved Jesus wholeheartedly, but who had a choleric character which he had never been able to conquer. Luther taught: "If you meet Moses, kill him." In another sense, Zen Buddhism says the same thing: "If you meet Buddha, kill him." I am not afraid of you, Moses. You are not allowed to stand in my way. I will fight you, and I will enter.

Do you oppose me with the tables of the commandments? But did you not smash them to pieces yourself? Paul also smashed them again. Did he not write that the tables of stone are done away?[6]

I remember vaguely that some church council branded as heresy antinomianism, the teaching that no moral law is any longer valid. But at this moment I am not particularly worried about church councils and their decisions.

I want forgiveness. I want justification. I want peace, whatever I have done in the past. The past is gone. I live in the present and the future, and the ghosts of the past are not permitted to haunt me. Neither are you permitted to torture me, setting my sin against the commandments. You did not respect them yourself. What right have you to play the moralist with me?

You are circling round me again, and yelling at me?

I can yell, too, and I will do it, even though I know that I shall be put in the strait-jacket again. Yes, I yell: "No sin is mine. All sin belongs to Jesus. It is he who has committed them all. Ask him, and he will confirm it. If you cannot forgive me my sins, if you are so wicked as to torture me every night in my helplessness, then forgive my sins to the one who has taken them on himself. Forgive my sins to Jesus. If you do not forgive him, he will not forgive you. And don't forget he has power to throw you into everlasting hell."

And now my last cry: "Yes, I have murdered, I have committed adultery, I lied, I was a heretic, but the blood of Jesus Christ washed me from all my sins and can wash you, too. Then you will become good, and will no more give pain to those whose victims you have been. Out! Out! I am baptised. I am washed in the blood of Jesus."

The guard has already put the key in the lock. Now I shall be gagged again. But the clock is striking one hour after midnight. Is it a coincidence? Is this the hour when you have to disappear? It cannot only be this. The blood of Jesus Christ has overcome you. I do not see you any more.

While they put the strait-jacket on, before they gag me, I cry out to you my final word: "You tortured me so much because you must be terribly tortured yourselves. Saints pray for those who have victimised them, instead of throwing mud at them. St. Joan of Arc, when she saw the Catholic bishop who had sentenced her to death approaching, cried: 'Beware that the flames may not endanger your life.' You are not saved. Believe in the blood of Jesus Christ. It will set you free." *Amen.*

Ani-hu

DEAR BROTHERS AND SISTERS

True knowledge of anything means as deep a union with your subject as that experienced in sexual intercourse. The knower, the known and the act of knowledge become one. You forget that you and your partner exist. You no longer think, but your mind is dissolved in the heat of the embrace.

It is perhaps in this sense that Meister Eckhart, the great German mystic, said that the Christian, in abandoning all things, must also abandon God. As long as you are still conscious of having a God, you have not yet become one with him.

The man who thinks and reasons about truth, shows by this that he does not possess it. Whoever has met King Truth, and has known his ardent kiss, does not seek the truth any longer, does not speak the truth, but is its very embodiment. Christ is no longer the object of your thoughts. You are his manifestation. Instead of being like Christ, you are identified with him. He is the light of the world. You are the light of the world. You are the same light.

St. Gertrude prayed: "I am you. You are I. I am not you, you are not I. I and you, we are a new being: an I-you."

Before I was put in the underground prison where I now am, I once stood at the window of my prison cell and cried: "Lord, where are you?" I had scarcely finished the last word, when I saw entering the prison yard my wife, with Bianca and another sister, who had come to inquire from the governor if I was in that prison. I had called to the Lord. Three sisters had come. Since then I have made it a habit to identify them and all true children of God with the Lord himself, and I know this is not a fancy.

Jesus himself identifies himself with us. "Whoever has fed, or given to drink, or clothed, or visited in prison one of these little brothers of mine, has done it to me."[1]

When Jesus met Saul of Tarsus, he asked him: "Saul, Saul, why persecutest thou me?"[2] Now the truth is that Saul had never persecuted Jesus. He had only persecuted the disciples. But Jesus knows no difference between himself and his disciples. When he speaks of his disciples, he does not use the third person. He says "me". He knows that I am he. And every Christian ought to know himself to be identical with Christ, a part of his mystical body.

So many people have helped me during my lifetime. I see the arm of the Almighty in all the arms which have been laid lovingly on my shoulder whenever I was depressed. God and the believing, good soul are one. Look at a believing soul, and you see the Lord himself.

Our Bibles translate Isaiah 48. 12 with the words: "I am he. I am the first, I also am the last." The Hebrew words are: "*Ani-hu ani harishon af ani haaharon*", which means, literally translated: "An 'I-he' (a union between me and him) is the first, and an 'I' (which is only I) is the last."

I was once looking for the Presbyterian pastor in a certain town. I went to the church, but the caretaker told me that he lived some distance away. Some boys were playing in the churchyard. Overhearing our conversation, one of them offered to show me the pastor's house. While we were walking along, I asked him if he believed in Christ. The boy, aged fourteen, decidedly answered: "No." I asked him why. He replied in his childish manner: "I believe that if God created this good and meek and loving Jesus of two thousand years ago in Palestine, in whom we are meant to trust, he must have created some little Jesus in every generation in every place, so that in looking at the little Jesus we may believe in the big one. But I have never met a little Jesus. I am a poor child. My father is a drunkard and beats me. My mother is a washer-woman and has no time for me. I have never had a good suit. Nobody has ever bought me chocolate or sweets. I have had no toys. If God is almighty, why did he only make Jesus once? An almighty God could make many Jesuses. Then it would be easy to believe." I asked him again: "But isn't your pastor a Jesus?" The answer was as decided as the first: "No."

And so we arrived at the pastor's house. The boy left. I was alone with the pastor. I spoke with him about Christ. It was an uninteresting subject for him. Then I told him what the boy had said. The pastor exclaimed: "What an idiot!" wherewith I whole-heartedly agreed. Only I considered somebody else to be the idiot.

To be a Christian means to be an "*Ani-hu*", an "I-he", an intimate union between a human soul and Christ. Jesus said to Philip: "Have I been so long time with you and yet hast thou not known me? He that hath seen me, hath seen the Father."[3] In the same way, a Christian can say to anyone who has known him for a long time: "He that has seen me, has seen Christ."

Humanity, in its religious development, has passed through the so-called animist period. Primitive man believed every object of nature to be possessed of a spirit. We have now left behind this stage of development, just as little girls stop playing with dolls at a certain age. A Christian sees things in a realistic manner and leaves dolls to children.

Dolls are made of plastic. They have no understanding. It is useless to speak to them and dress them up. The brides of the heavenly king do not populate their minds with the objects of their imagination. We look cold reality straight in the face. We prisoners have cried out in our pain for years, without getting any answer. So many of the Lord's vineyards have been destroyed. The Lord has hidden his face from us.

As savages saw spirits behind every tree and in every stone, it is our sick imagination which evokes in our mind the presence of Jesus. Some see him in the bread and wine of Holy Communion and believe that a transubstantiation has occurred, or at least a consubstantiation as the Lutherans put it. We do not wish to acknowledge freely that the Heavenly King is not there. We cry in vain, as he cried in vain: "My God, my God, why hast thou forsaken me?"

He is beyond the wall of partition which we ourselves have created between him and us by our sins. Beyond the wall are the angels. Only cold light comes from the stars, and dark thoughts whiten my hair.

It is so cold in the cell. I am nearly frozen. The only living companion I had for a short while, a spider, froze. I live in a cold universe.

The only place where there is still life is deep within me. But is he not there? Is it not true that the one whom I seek in vain in the outward world, breaks the ice of silence in me; that Christ and God are in me, that my voice, my whispers or my yells which provoke the guards to reprisals, are their whispers and their yells?

Christ has promised that he will come to dwell in those who keep his commandments. I did not keep them fully but, notwithstanding, he came. He is much more generous than his word. Or perhaps with him remorse at not fulfilling the commandments is the same as fulfilling them.

Perhaps there is something else. I think he must have been bored in his empty heaven. I am his real heaven. Heaven is no heaven for him without me and others like me. And so he came. But he came.

I am an *Ani-hu*. This gives me an enormous power to do good. In me is the living God.

Like St. Peter, I would exclaim: "Lord, it is good for us to be here!"[4] It is much better with you here in prison than when I was in the pulpit. Then I preached so many sermons and wrote so many books about you, that you had come to be a habit with me. I spoke and wrote so easily about Christian things that I had no need to pay attention to you.

And so you took me to the peak of the mountain, that is to this underground cell. Here you, and those who now take pleasure in gagging me even if I don't yell, taught me silence. So the startling thing happened, the mystical union, the realisation of *Ani-hu*.

Seek to attain this, my beloved brothers. *Amen.*

Sick of Love

JESUS

In a luxurious bedroom embellished with flowers, in a kingly palace, a rather theatrical setting for love, the bride of the Song of Songs waited for Solomon to come.

We are sick of love for you in our prison cells.

She was surrounded by girls to wait on her. We are surrounded only by hatred and wickedness. Every day they mock and beat and torture us. It is years since I saw a man who loves me, or heard one single good word.

Jesus, leap over the mountains which separate us and come to your beloved ones! We perish. The spirit within us was quenched long ago. We don't have your Holy Book. Our eyes weep tears day and night.

Is it right that the One who cried, "My God, my God, why hast Thou forsaken me?", who knew himself the anguish of loneliness, should forsake us?

Jesus, a broken heart cries out to you. I am weary. Give me rest. You who can change a hell into paradise, who by the one word "I will" made a leper clean, give me quiet. Solomon gave maidens to wait on his bride. Give me angels to surround me, but, I beg you, angels whom I can see, not angels whose presence I always have to imagine.

Until a few weeks ago, I had at least the consolation of bringing souls to Christ by tapping the Gospel in morse code through the wall. The guards have found it out. And now they have emptied the cells on my right and on my left. My self has become entirely useless. I sit and wait for the passing away of this senseless life which consists in eating dirty soup twice a day, and enduring boring beatings. Even these no longer have the thrill of novelty. The torturers have no imagination. The pains they inflict on us are always the same. They are senseless, too, because I have forgotten everything and could not tell them any secrets of the Underground church, even if I wanted to.

What people seek most in religion is to keep their self in eternity. I would like to get rid of my self and to become "you". If I lie sick of love and wait for you to come, it is not in the hope that you will give my self, which I abhor, eternal life, but that you will take it from me. There will then be in my place another being, one like you, one full of grace and truth.

In the past, I would spend hours thinking of what I would do if I were a king, a beggar, a millionaire, a girl, what I would do if I were the Pope, or the ruler of my country.

Now I dream more and more about what I will do when I am like you. Will I have to suffer again, even worse than now? You had a heaven and left it, because on a speck of dust in your infinite universe there was a tiny creature, man, and this creature suffered. What if there should be suffering or rebellion again somewhere in what is wrongly called the universe (I would rather call it a pluriverse. It is so big and varied)? I would feel like you, and I would come to suffer for those who had rebelled. I would bear the infirmities of others, and take their sickness upon me. The prophecies of Isaiah would refer to me too.[1]

I was once your disciple. Then I became a worker in your harvest. There are three degrees in Christianity as in every profession, as in masonry. From being a disciple and worker, you advance to the higher degree. I have to become, like St. Paul, a "master builder".[2]

Woe to the disciples who never become workers, to the workers who never become masters. They are like perpetual students who never become doctors or engineers. What is the use of a violin player who does not try to become a virtuoso?

So you have brought me to prison to make me a master. But while the disciples dance after a day of labour, and the workers sleep, the master stays up late into the night to plan future work and to care for everything necessary. Masters have no peace. Will I, too, never have peace?

No, I cannot become like you if I continue to think these things. Was it by thinking that you became a man of sorrows? Or did it come to you in the simplest manner, through accepting what the Father willed for you?

The Catholic church says that you have a high opinion of scholastic theologians, that when St. Thomas Aquinas finished his *Summa Theologica* he heard your voice from heaven saying: "You have written well of me, Thomas."

To me they are all unacceptable. They made the truth too clear-cut. Of course, they could not know Heisenberg's theory of the indeterminacy of elementary particles. The standard of measurement changes the object measured. This is not only true in microphysics. A God whom I love is different from one who is unloved. With the pure, He is pure, with the froward, froward.[3] There is no absolute truth. Truth is a direction, not an attainment. The truth about God is different for every man.

But anyhow, the scholastic theologians made a difference between what they called in Latin *mens agens* (the active mind) and *mens patiens* (the passive mind). The active mind will pass through valleys, mountains and caves to find the truth. The passive mind lies sick of love and, like a magnetic tape, simply records what it hears.

While other Christians go forth to battle, the masters, those with passive minds, remain quietly in the most holy place of the temple. They know that a God who has to be defended by me, a God whose holy ark can be overthrown by oxen so that I have to keep it in its right place, is not worthy of the name "God".

You need no defenders. You need no men armed with sticks to fight your cause. What you seek is worshippers in the highest sense, that is, lovers – men who love you, serenely and quietly, whatever is happening around and in them.

You seek for souls in whom are rest, quietness, immovability, for only these can mirror the splendours of heaven.

You were so greatly beloved by God because you mirrored in serenity his glory. You did not fear that you would become a man of sorrows. You did not even think about it. *"Ehjeh asher ehjeh,"* said God to Moses.[4] This may be translated not only as "I am what I am." It can also have the meaning, "I will become what I will become." When you are a son of God you become quietly whatever you become by the will of the Father and by the working of his laws. The source becomes a river, the egg becomes a bird, the bud a flower, the living being a corpse, the still sea becomes tempestuous, the tempestuous sea still. There is nothing to think about. I develop towards becoming you, as a caterpillar develops towards becoming a butterfly. *"Ehjeh asher ehjeh."* I will become what the laws of the divine nature of which I am a partaker will make me become. The caterpillar becomes what the law of his nature makes him become.

I was always so active. Finding no other means of achieving your aim, you arranged for me to have fifty-pound chains on my legs so that I am obliged to sit quietly at your feet, like Mary of Bethany.

The active mind always returns from its hunting parties empty-handed, like Esau, while Jacob, the passive mind, remaining at home, can buy Esau's birthright with a mouthful of soup.

Quietness is the antidote to all the sorrows of this life. It is also the antidote to the sorrows of prison life and a shield against the fear of future suffering.

Fighting is for those who are still caught up in the vanity of this world. In my subterranean cell I remain like Moses on the mountain top. I cannot keep my hands stretched upwards. I am too weak for this. I am alone. I have no Aaron or Hur to hold up my arms. But I stretch my heart upwards, and know that thus Israel becomes unconquerable.

I will lie sick of a burning love and make no effort to think what I will do when I become you. There is nothing in my cell to stimulate the active mind. The passive mind simply rethinks in quietness a thought which was thought long since by God.

We play back what was recorded on our minds long ago by the Holy Spirit.

Thank you, dear Jesus, for putting me in this solitary cell with the purpose of making me a master mind. Thank you for the paralysing sickness of love. I wish for nothing else than that my self should pass away and that my last breath should take the shape of one more flower in the garland wherewith you are beautified. And if it should be the fate of this flower to wither away on another Golgotha, I have no need to worry about it now.

Now, I only love. *Amen.*

The Fullest Sabbath

MY DEAR SOUL

I must be really mad.

While I was free I visited many asylums for the insane. With some of the madmen one could have very pleasant conversations. Some of them were men of exceptional intelligence. Only sometimes, suddenly, they would give way for a time to unreasonable behaviour, which did not last for long.

I am reduced to the self-diagnosis of someone who is not a psychiatrist. No doctor has been to see me to tell me what is happening to me. Sometimes I am afraid of my lucidity. I have the impression not only that I can see and understand things rightly but that I can see right through them. As a matter of fact, I direct the interrogations. I make the interrogator ask me the questions that I like. I always succeed in diverting him from subjects where I am not at ease. I entice him into discussions lasting for many hours about the relationship between Marxism and Christianity, until he forgets why he has called me. I feel that I could preach or write books as never before. And then, all at once, my mind becomes confused, darkened, filled with mad thoughts. I begin to yell without any obvious motive. I bang on the door of the cell crying: "Give me back my Mihai. Give me back my son."

Things seem to be getting worse and worse. It is a Sabbath day. This time I am not only in a strait-jacket and gagged but I have heavy chains at my feet which prevent me from walking. A Sabbath day. The fullest Sabbath I have ever enjoyed in my life. I cannot disturb my rest even by a movement of my hands, feet or lips.

At first I felt an impulse to ask God, as St. Theresa asked

him: "Why do you treat us so? I don't wonder that you have not many friends." I wanted to tell God: "You may do everything in your power to destroy my trust and my love towards you, but you will not succeed." But then I decided to give him a rest. Let him also enjoy a full Sabbath, undisturbed by any reproaches of mine.

I will once again speak only to you, my soul, my only treasure. I hope this is not blasphemy, because I believe you to be one with Christ – with Christ who has humbled himself again, to be sin and man full of frailties within me. You are he, and therefore you are the jewel. In any case, I have no bishop, no theologians, no church elders to censor what I think. So I call you just what I like, my only treasure.

Enter into Sabbath, my soul. Overcome your anxieties and doubts. Your sins are forgiven. Not only the past sins but the future ones, too. If you don't believe me, believe Spurgeon. He also put it exactly like this. Although I wonder why you should believe Spurgeon more than me. Enter into Sabbath, my soul. You are saved from the fear of judgment. You don't even have to judge yourself. You can think about yourself entirely objectively, as if you were somebody else.

It is understood, forgiven, you must not worry about it, but it is simply not right that so much of your worship has been honouring God with my lips only, the heart remaining far from him. I don't reproach you for it. It could not be otherwise. Jesus said: "The hour is coming, and now is . . ."[1] We are not all of one piece. While for a part of our soul the hour to worship in spirit and in truth is already here, for another part it is still to come. Luther taught that we are "*simul justus et peccator, comprehensor et viator*"(at the same time righteous and sinners, men who have attained the goal and travellers towards it). I do not ask you, my soul, to judge and condemn yourself but rather to strive to love and worship with all your heart, with all your soul.

But, having in my heart both good and bad inclinations, how can I love God with all my heart? The answer of the Kabbala, the ancient mystic teaching of the Jewish people, is: "Serve

God also with your bad impulses, then you will serve him whole-heartedly." If you understand, you understand. If you don't, no explanation will help.

But your religion must become a full reality. Even if you quarrel with God, as David and Job quarrelled with Him under similar circumstances, it must be a deeply religious, whole-hearted quarrel.

The prodigal son, when he returned home, did not stop at the house of an aunt, or a neighbour. He went through to the Father. Even to stop at Jesus is wrong. Jesus teaches that through him you must arrive at the Father, the Most High, the God of gods, the highest point of Jacob's ladder.

"Religion" comes from a Latin word which means "to tie again". Do you feel so tied to God, as I am tied in this strait-jacket and chains, that you cannot move unless he unties you?

Don't let words take the place of reality. In Hebrew, *"davar"* is a homonym which means "word" and "thing". The genius of the Hebrew language demands that words should be things. Don't forget, my soul, that it is your privilege to be a Jewish soul. Here, among the "internationalist" Communists, who had as the founder of their party an anti-semitic Jew, Marx, it means one more beating. But before God it means a great deal, and lays upon you a special responsibility.

Don't stay in the sphere of words and names. The name of one of the high priests who killed Jesus was Annas, which means in Hebrew "pity". And what a ruthless man he was!

Understand me well, my soul. I don't judge you, nor do I reproach you. Self-judgments are always false. Life is very complicated, and we always err in such judgments by applying to life only one criterion. In justice, human actions should be valued according to many criteria.

A word may not be truthful but it may be useful. It is rumoured that at the Teheran conference Churchill said: "Truth is so precious that it has to be surrounded by a numerous bodyguard of lies." A sentence dreadful to read. But I wonder who could win a war with military or diplomatic weapons without using deception. St. Paul used it when, after calling the high priest a "whitewashed wall" and putting him under a curse, he apologised, saying that he had not known him to be the high priest. He used deception when, in order to divide the Pharisees and Sadducess, he cried: "I am a Pharisee . . . with respect to the hope and the resurrection of the dead I am on trial," which was not at all the issue.[2] He used deception, or if you prefer a milder word, diplomacy, in circumcising Timothy, although he had written that whoever practices the Jewish ritual falls from grace. There are other words of ours whose aim is not to impart truth but to lift men into the realm of mystery; others again may embellish life, or make it easier to bear. This is the case with works of art, and with funny stories. Some words may not be true, but they may be a valuable means of self-defence and of defending the innocent. Such are the words with which I lead astray my interrogators. There exist not only truth and lies. There are also intermediate stages between them.

Humility is sometimes right, and wrong at other times. What a catastrophe if Koch, the discoverer of the tubercle bacillus, had been humble enough to give in when all the members of the academies of science contested his discovery! He was self-asserting. So also was St. Athanasius. You cannot detect, in his debate with Arius the heretic, even the slightest sign of humility. In vain will you seek for it in Wycliff or Luther.

You cannot judge human actions according to isolated criteria like truthfulness, love, humility, or religiosity.

And then there is in our psyche an objective law. I cannot always do the things I want to do. There are natural reactions and impulses which I cannot master, as I cannot master the beating of my heart, the working of my kidneys and the movement of stars in the skies. They are not submitted to my will. Ancestral forces are battling within me. I am the descendant of men who for two thousand years have refused Christianity. It is not easy to implant it in a soul fighting against such an inheritance.

I don't judge you, nor condemn you, my soul, but I lay before you this noble task: be whole-heartedly Christian.

How? I really don't know. You can easily recognise false teachers by the fact that they know the answers to all the questions.

But perhaps my actual state could be an indication for you: enter into full Sabbath. Don't move at all, as I do not move. Lao Tse recommended inaction as the highest type of action.

Simply trust, knowing that Jesus holds in his hands the bridle of the ass.

I will tell you a story.

A preacher went on Palm Sunday to preach to a congregation of cowboys, who were used to taming wild horses. When he had finished telling how Jesus entered into Jerusalem on a foal which nobody had ridden before, and how he was received with shouts of joy and men waving palm-branches, the cowboys surrounded him, exclaiming: "Jesus was one of us! He too was a cowboy!" The preacher did not understand, so the cowboys explained: "If you rode on a donkey which nobody had ridden before, and thousands of people around you were shouting and waving branches in the donkey's face, you, pastor, would have finished up under the donkey! If Jesus could keep his donkey quiet, believe us, he had the strong hand and the skill of the cowboy."

Just leave the bridle in the hands of Jesus. He has made saints out of murderers and thieves. He can make you a saint, also, provided you leave him alone. It is the Sabbath. Don't hate. Always be like I am, gagged, only speaking out when it is for the honour of the Lord and for the good of His work.

It is the fullest Sabbath imaginable. Don't even be afraid of error. You are a pawn in the hands of a master chess-player. He will not lose the game.

Leave your remorse, the terrible "ifs": "If only I had acted otherwise." You could not have done otherwise. There is no free will. You are what heredity, education, social environment and the influences of good and bad angels have made you. In the last analysis, this means that at every stage of your development you are exactly what God meant you to be at that moment.

Leave your doubts. Life is incalculable. We don't know even

one atom of the five octillions of atoms which make up our body. We don't know our genes. We don't know the complexities of our souls, nor what happens in our subconscious. You can remain in Sabbath only by trusting that your life has been calculated by the one who knows every drop of rain and every hair on my head. Every step of our pilgrim life is counted.

Trust in Him, even if He slays me. This is the only advice I can give you. *Amen.*

There Is No God

(A MEDITATION)

Our oppressors say: "There is no God." The Communists ask us, too, to deny God as a condition of our release.

I wonder if I should not do it.

Our experiences in Communist prisons have helped us to understand many parts of the Bible in a new way. I do not agree that we should consider all atheists fools because David wrote: "The fool hath said in his heart, there is no God."[1] First of all, even according to the Bible, it is only the man who says it in his heart who is a fool. He deserves the name because he does not say openly what he thinks. We cannot widen the use of the term to describe those who sincerely and openly tell us that their experience of life has made them convinced atheists.

The faith of some Christians around me has been destroyed by the weight of suffering. Job said: "Oh that my grief were thoroughly weighed, and my calamity laid in the balances together! For now it would be heavier than the sand of the sea . . ."[2] Now there are once again prisoners in the adjoining cells. One Christian prisoner has just read me – in morse code – a short poem entitled "God, I forgive thee". He composed it after passing through terrible torture. Others find more ease for their mind in simply denying that God exists, instead of accusing him or forgiving him. I cannot call these men fools.

And then, the facts of science known to us today were not known in David's time. Some modern scientists, analysing the facts, have come to faith. Others in the same laboratory, having the same facts before them, have become atheists. In justice, we must say that the material reality is open to interpretation in both ways, just as there are two theories of the nature of light. Is it fair that one set of scientists should call the other a bunch of fools?

I believe. My Communist oppressor does not. That is all. He is an oppressor and I am not. But I have my sins which he has not, and these may be much more heinous than his. St. Paul considered himself the chief of sinners. I believe him when he says this, as I believe him in other things. It was he who was the chief of sinners, not Annas or Caiaphas, not Judas, not the Roman torturers and executioners. St. Paul knew facts about his own life which we do not know. He also knew all the horrible deeds of those who were responsible for the death of the Son of God. There was no false humility in him. If, after comparing what he knew about himself with what he knew about these others, he said that he was the chief of sinners, I have no reason to disagree with him.

Probably, the brothers who are free look on me as a martyr. They think of sermons which they have heard me preach. They have read some of my books. They have had pleasant talks with me. They don't know me. I know myself. I am no better than my torturers. Only my sins are in a different category.

The opinions of the oppressor are as valid as those of the oppressed. He disbelieves. I believe. He has the same rights as I. I cannot call him a fool.

Deny God? There is a sense in which any Christian can do it.

The great mystic teacher Meister Eckhart taught that a disciple of Jesus, after having left all for love of him, must at the end leave God, too. This seems to me to be self-evident. In the supreme moment of sexual union, those who are united are not conscious of the separate existence of the partner. In supreme moments of mystic union, I, the thinker, God, the object of my thoughts and the act of thinking become one. This is the fulfilment of "Hear, O Israel, the Lord thy God is one." It is only the man who has not yet united with God who has a God. In a sense, there is a religious atheism, transcending the stage in which a man has a God.

What have I asserted when I say that "God is"?

St. John Chrysostom said that the expression "God" is not the name of his being or of his existence, and that it is not possible to find the proper name of that being. St. Augustine says that it is not lawful to call God even "the inexpressible", because even by this you express something about Him.

Maimonides, and many others with him, thought that the best way to know God is the *via negationis*, the way of negation, that is to deny everything about him which can be put in human words.

When Moffatt went as a missionary to Africa, he wished to explain a train to the natives who only knew the ox-cart. So he put two pieces of wood on the ground, to symbolise the rails. He put a few carts one behind the other. To the first cart he hitched a pair of oxen, and hung a steam kettle round the neck of one animal. This, he explained, represented a train. If anyone of his hearers had been bold enough to deny the existence of such a thing, he would have been right, and not the missionary.

So it is with God. Those who deny what we assert about God may be nearer to the truth than we are.

Human words grew out of the necessity for men to communicate with each other in hunting, cultivation or marriage. Then we projected words on to the spiritual realm, which is totally different. Words are inadequate – the word "God", too.

A monk once agreed with a brother that the one who died first would try to come back to describe what it is like in the other world. The first to die fulfilled his promise. When the living man asked him in Latin, "*qualiter?*" (how is it?), the answer was "*totaliter aliter*" (entirely otherwise).

Christians use words for the best attributes of God. About some other attributes – for example his terribleness ("the terror of the Lord" as the Bible calls it) and his revengefulness, they prefer to be silent, because they think that what is ugly in a human character must be unfit for God, too, a thought which I consider stupid. Many things which would be a shame for a child are allowable in a man. God cannot be put into words.

"The expressed Tao (God) is not the real Tao," says Lao-Tse.

If the Communists see in God only a word, and I myself do not believe in the word either, why not deny him and be free?

Formally, I would be right to do it, and I would do it if I did not fear that, by doing so, I would cause the most harm to my oppressors.

If I say "there is no God", towards what will they develop? What will be the aim of their life? The Bible says that when Christ will appear we shall be like him, and that those who overcome will sit with Christ and God on the same throne. I am developing towards Godhead, as the embryo develops towards man. If there were no man in the whole world but only one male and one female child, you could not say that mankind did not exist. There would soon be a man. If I develop rightly, there will soon be a Christ, a godly being, sitting on a heavenly throne.

If I deny God I cause my torturer to lose such an opportunity for development. I leave him no aim in life, and cause him to lose his soul, with the huge potentialities hidden within it.

The Hindus call God "No, No," in the sense that he is nothing of what we presume him to be. Even if there is no God, I will think only about him, about how a world with God would be. I will never forsake God as my aim.

I owe it to my Communist torturers to confess to them in words which they can understand the one who is mystery for myself, about whom nobody can tell the "when" and the "how", who is inaccessible, incomprehensible even to religious geniuses, and who can reveal himself only in the etymological sense of the word "re-veal", that is to put another veil upon his face by reducing himself to the ridiculously humble sphere of words.

No, I will not deny him. My mind does not know who he is or where he is. When I was strung up by my arms with my toes barely reaching the floor, and under other similar tortures, I had no evidence that he exists. I was inclined to accuse him as St. Theresa, the great Christian mystic, dared to accuse him before me: "O Lord, no wonder you have so few friends when you treat them so hard." But I believe in the incomprehensible and terrible one. I believe that he is love, although at this moment I feel nothing of his love. I have to believe in its expression in a sacrifice two thousand years ago. I will not leave him, nor deny him, even if he leaves me.

The Unreasonableness of
Love

DEAR BROTHERS AND SISTERS

I once met a woman who was a missionary in Africa. She was renowned for her extreme zeal in the service of the people. At first, we chatted on the surface of things. Then deep spoke to deep. I was able to ask her: "What is it that prevents you from sitting down quietly to pass hours and days with the Christ whom you love? What drives you to leave him and rush into outward activity?"

I had touched a sore point. She admitted she was over-zealous because she was not sure of the rightness of what she was doing. She told me: "Jesus said, 'If ye were blind, ye should have no sin.'[1] I went to a blind people, Muslims who, not knowing about Christ, did not have the sin of unbelief. God could not reproach them for their wrong belief, since they had not heard of a better one. Now I tell them about Christ. With almost no exception, they refuse my message. But they have heard it. So their sin remains. By my missionary activity I am doing them harm rather than good. It is impossible to convert Muslims. Then why burden them with a knowledge which they cannot accept?"

She loved those Muslim people. But she had brought her love and her concern for their salvation to the bar of reason. Once you allow reason, which Luther called "the beast", to judge feelings, feelings are always defeated. From the point of view of reason Romeo was a fool. How can you prove to reason that it is right to die for a Juliet when in Verona there are thousands of Rosalindas who are just as charming?

Reason will tell you about the foolishness of the cross. Jesus was young, handsome, vigorous. He could have made a good living as a carpenter, or as a doctor of the law. He could have married, and enjoyed life, and still remained religious and a philanthropist. Why die to save people who do not want to be saved? Why start a religion which will not be accepted, or even heard of, by the overwhelming majority of mankind, and which will be practised only by a few isolated saints?

Who would conceive such an unreasonable project? Only St. Paul dared to answer this question. A chill runs down your spine when you hear the answer. This plan of salvation arose from "the foolishness of God".[2] The Bible is the only religious book to contain such an expression, which must surely be considered a blasphemy by all the religions of the world, including Christianity – "the foolishness of God!"

Love must submit to being condemned by reason. I told my missionary friend: "Just follow the promptings of love. Don't try to justify your actions by arguments."

We in prison use the same unreasonableness. When we hear the cries of someone being beaten, all the others begin to bang on their doors, crying: "Help! Help! Stop beating!" There is nobody to hear us, except those who are beating and who now, instead of beating only one, beat us all up, one after the other. You hear the doors being unlocked. Now it is the fourth prisoner to my right. Follows the third. I have only two left. Then I hear the cries of my nearest neighbour. Only two or three minutes left – how long these minutes are – and then I will be beaten, too. What is the sense of a collective protest here? What is the sense of expressing your solidarity with those who are beaten? It is non-sense, which means that it is pure love. Love does not think about what it will achieve, what it will gain. Love does not think at all. Love does not care about reason. Why should it?

If we are to love our enemies, why should we not love reason, that bitter critic, too? We can succeed in doing this. But we shall never persuade reason to love love. Reason considered Jesus and Paul to be madmen. My reason condemns me as mad, too.

This time I attained a paroxysm of unreasonableness. When

the guards entered to give me my share of the beating I jumped at one of them and kicked him. I am so thin. They are so many. It was foolish. Reason tells me: "Christ taught you to turn the other cheek." I answer: "Shut up! I have to turn the other cheek when I am slapped, not when my brother is tortured and my whole nation is oppressed."

Now I am punished to stay, I don't know for how long, in a cell I have known about for some time. It is full of dozens of rats which, being hungry, jump around, not allowing me to sleep.

I have just passed the first hours here. I am not tired. I watch the rats and am reminded of Heisenberg's law of the undeterminacy of elementary particles. (How foolish to think about physics in such circumstances.) When you boil water, you know that the mass of molecules as a whole enters into quicker movement. But what each single molecule will do is unpredictable. Some continue to move at the old speed, and some even slow down their movements. I observe the same thing happening with the rats. I had thought about them as a species. But rats are also individuals, and each one has a character of its own. Some are running around looking for food which does not exist. Some are trying to gnaw the rags I have on my feet. I don't even drive them away. Some are gnawing their own tails. Some seem like philosophers, resigned. They sit quietly and wait for their death. They have given up the search.

Dear rats! It is written: "The young lions roar after their prey, and seek their meat from God."[3] And God gives them their meat. Sometimes he gives them as meat the bodies of his saints. And why not? If a saint eats the meat of a guiltless lamb in a religious ceremony, why should not his own turn come, and his own guiltless life be eaten up by a lion? Shouldn't you, rats, also seek your meat from God? I used to recite in church every Sunday that God is the maker of all things, visible and invisible. So he is your maker too, although I don't see the slightest reason why rats should exist. But neither do the Communists see any reason why Wurmbrand should exist. God's thoughts are not my thoughts.

It is said that St. Francis of Assisi made the birds praise God at his command. St. Anthony of Padua is supposed to have called the fish near to the shore to listen to his sermons. What about rats?

Ha, ha, ha! Here you have it, Richard. Your jailers are right to put you in a strait-jacket occasionally. You are definitely mad. Everything you have just said is sheer foolishness. I agree, but I only ask myself if it is not "the foolishness of God".

I don't ask you, reason, if my love and care should extend to rats, too. I too would say that they should be exterminated. They eat the crops needed by us men. They would say: "The farmers eat the crops needed by us rats." But then they are carriers of disease. I wonder how they would defend themselves for that.

My mind is getting more and more confused. Probably I shall yell soon.

My mind jumps about from molecules to rats. Now it has forgotten the rats and thinks about Western Christians. I remember the tragic word in Philippians: "No church communicated with me."[4] Why are we abandoned by the Western Christians?

Their reason, probably, tells them that they could do nothing practical for us. But why do they follow reason, which Luther called "the beast" and not love? Why don't they come to free us, with the risk that they will be defeated and suffer the same fate as us? Their strategists may tell them that the balance of power is not in their favour. But since when has love consulted strategists? Why does not a group of a thousand Western Christians come as tourists, attack our prison, rush into the corridors and tell us: "We have not forgotten you. We love you"? It may be a foolish enterprise. But from our side it was also a foolish thing to bang on a cell door when our brother was beaten.

And then, the Western Christians all have their guardian angels. Each has six wings, which means that they are prepared to fetch messages. Why don't they send their guardian angels to caress our weary heads and to tell us about love? I feel the nearness of such angels, but when I ask them where they come from they are nearly always from another prison cell or from a brother in Rumania itself. Can angels from the West be stopped at the Iron Curtain? How big are their wings? Are they the wings of a chicken, which cannot fly, or the wings of an eagle?

Where is the unreasonableness of love? If these Christians are partakers of the divine nature, why are they not also partakers of the foolishness of God?

Foolish questions, dear brothers and sisters. If I spoke to you tonight it was to teach you one thing: dare to walk in the foolish, completely unreasonable, paths of love! St. Augustine said: "Love God, and do what you will." Love, and your foolish actions will be wiser than the wisdom of men. *Amen.*

The Lesson of the Cell
with the Rats

DEAR BROTHERS AND SISTERS

Communication between us was interrupted for a while.

God, in ancient times, sent an angel who shut the lions' mouths so that they did not hurt Daniel. I am sure he did the same for me. The angel was sent. But angels are unpredictable beings. If on their way they see a flower whose petals are weighed down by heavy rain, they will stop to put the flower straight again. They will pause to dry someone's tears, or to help an overburdened donkey to carry its load. If they meet a child, they stop to caress him. My angel did not arrive in time. The mouths of the rats were not shut. Because of them, I could not concentrate.

Happily, I did not stay with them long, only for forty-eight hours. Then I was taken back downstairs to my own cell. Going down to it was like approaching heaven.

It was no mystery to me that heaven was below rather than above.

I once had a vision of being led to heaven. I had thought until then that heaven was above. But a beautiful female angel who lovingly showed me the way explained to me that, because heaven was too high for many to reach, because so many could not bear the cold of the heavenly peaks, heaven descended in the person of Jesus Christ until it was lower than every lowness. However low a man may have fallen, heaven is even lower. A man can be in heaven not only in moments of sublime rapture but also when he commits a gross sin. The publican who said in the temple: "God, be merciful to me, a sinner," went down to his house justified.[1] Nowhere are we told that he ceased to be a publican. He never voiced such a desire. But, because he prayed rightly, heaven descended below him, to the level of publicans who were worse extortioners than he. He could be in heaven, while still remaining, for a time at least, a publican.

So I found it quite natural that the cell with the rats should be above, and that my own cell, this beautiful place of serenity, should be below.

My quiet cell to which I descend is a higher heaven. But even the cell with the rats is not outside heaven. "In God we live and move."[2] If in God we move, Christians who are moved into torture cells and out of them again never leave God and his heaven.

How can even a cell with rats be heaven? It is about this that I want to speak to you today.

Jesus said on the cross: "My God, my God, why didst thou forsake me?"[3] Notice carefully the tense of the verb. He did not say: "Why dost thou forsake me?" He used the past tense. He was speaking of an episode already in the past, not of what was happening at that moment. But was it not at that moment that God had forsaken him, because he had become the personification of sin? Was not the cross, Golgotha, the place of forsakenness?

Yes, but I experienced the days with the rats not as the present, but as a past to which I looked back. Not only did I believe that we, Christians, are seated in heavenly places. My faith – or, if you prefer it, my imagination, or my madness – showed me many heavenly places of indescribable beauty. I chose a site, and deliberately sat down. It was a "green bed",[4] and beside me was "my beloved, fair and pleasant". This heavenly place, filled with delights, was my present state in the cell of the rats, and will remain my state in all eternity. Then what about the rats? They could only be my past. I looked on their gnawing as on a past suffering which worried me, my real being, my spirit, as little as the spanking which I had received from my mother thirty-five years earlier. It was over and done with.

That is why Jesus, while on the cross he was passing through the worst of sufferings – being forsaken by his God – used the past tense. He said that he had been forsaken, not that he was forsaken at that moment.

Every man can construct a future for himself, even if it is only "a castle in Spain". But an imaginary castle in Spain is a very real castle. You can sometimes be much happier in it than the owners of real castles are.

In the same way I can construct for myself an imaginary past (except that I don't consider it as imaginary, but as a spiritual reality), and I can situate the present suffering, the cross or the cell with the rats, in this past. Huss, Cranmer and other saints in heaven no longer feel the pain of being burned at the stake, because this belongs to the past. Jesus no longer feels the pain of being scourged and nailed to the cross. Golgotha is a past episode of his eternal life. And he lived it as a past even when he was on Golgotha.

I would build too much on the fact that the verb *sabachthani* is in the past tense, if it were not for my own experience and that of many Christian sufferers. There is a "religious anaesthesia". It was this that enabled Paul and Silas to sing after a heavy beating and with their feet in the stocks.

And then there followed another stage. The rats may have remained so far as my body was concerned, and perhaps the lower faculties of simple aperception of the soul. My knowledge of them disappeared.

At the marriage feast in Cana, Jesus changed water into wine. What sort of wine? It is recorded that he changed it into "good wine". The ruler of the feast said: "Thou hast kept the good wine until now."[5] Only old wine is good wine. So he did not change the water into new wine. He made it to have been wine already for many years. You don't become a saint when you are converted. Jesus changes water into old wine. He makes the harlot Magdalene to have always been a saint. He does not make the torture cease at a certain moment. He makes the torture never to have begun. He does not seat you in holy places the moment you realise it practically. He makes it that you have always been seated there.

Men can change for good or evil the present or the future of their fellow-men. Jesus is the only one who can change the past. So the cell with the rats no longer existed, even in the past. The spirit had detached itself from outward reality and enjoyed the Bridegroom.

When they unlocked the door to take me out, I awoke. I saw the rats. I was afraid, and thought it would be heaven to be taken out of there. But it was only for a few minutes that I was out of heaven, while the guards unlocked the door, entered and made me come back to what they call reality and what I consider to be just a nightmare.

Live actual sorrows as though they were past. Believe that Jesus has changed your whole past, wiping out of it everything that is ugly and sad. This is the key to happiness, and I found it in the blessed cell with the rats.

It is this discovery that I wished to share with you. *Amen.*

Talk with My Son Mihai

MIHAI

When the holy virgin entered into Elisabeth's house, her babe leaped for joy. Was this something exceptional? Do babies understand? In Yugoslavia a few years ago a miracle child was born, who spoke and answered questions at six weeks. The Bible says: "Out of the mouth of babes and sucklings thou hast perfected praise."[1]

In any case, your mother and I talked to you about God from the time you were a baby. We believed that you would understand.

Now you are eleven. Now you certainly understand. You know how much I love you. For hours on end I caress my pillow and talk to it, imagining that it is you. Jesus said that a piece of baker's bread was his body, and that wine bought from a pub was his blood. Why can't my pillow be you? Every material object can support a spiritual reality. Jesus is a door and light and a lion and a lamb. Spiritual realities can express themselves through all kinds of things, even contradictory ones.

As I embrace the pillow it becomes warm, and then I have the same feeling as I had when I pressed your body to mine when you were small. I sing and talk to you. The pillow becomes the conductor through which love streams from me to you. No, it is not the conductor. Here again reason is trying to set right my feelings. It is you, you yourself.

Mihai, the end has arrived. I cannot bear it any more. I have saved thirty pills. The torture has become too painful. I am afraid that I will crack. I will take the pills and go to the one whom you once, as a child of five, saw walking through the room. I will go to that one who said: "I am the resurrection and the life."[2]

He never forbade suicide. He could not. He himself committed a sophisticated form of suicide. He said it himself: "No man taketh my life from me . . . I lay down my life for the sheep." He provoked his own death. He asked wolves to become lambs, which is not in their power. The only possible result, which he foresaw, was that the wolves had to devour him. His intention was that, devoured by them, he might produce from within the change which nobody can make of his own free will.

He will understand my suicide. And you will understand it one day, too, even if not for many years. You will have to remain fatherless, as I was left without a father at the age of nine.

I read somewhere that ninety per cent of famous men were orphan children. You complained to me once: "Father, you know the answers to all my questions. You stop me thinking for myself because you are always right." I will no longer stand in the way of your development. My suicide can work for your good.

My last word to you, Mihai, is: "Love the Lord Jesus." You cannot do without him.

We have a telegraph system that functions perfectly from cell to cell. So we learn that the Communists are putting more and more of their own people in prison. These are men who have sinned against Communist ethics, against the rules of the Party. The Communists also have their moral code. It demands full obedience to the Party line. Everyone acknowledges a moral code. Thieves share fairly what they have stolen together. Torturers hold it their duty to be ruthless against the class enemy. And everyone disobeys his moral law. It is a fact that Goering, the killer of millions of Jews, saved the life of one Jewish family. He was not loyal to his anti-semitism. Our guards sometimes do us some little favour, or disobey the Party line in some other manner, just as Christians accept the Christian standard, but sin in one matter or another. Nobody can avoid sin. Even if a man's religion were the devil's own, with the firm decision to commit every mortal sin daily, he would sometimes have a moment of weakness and allow one possible victim to escape. So he would sin against his religion.

I don't know what your future religious development will be. Perhaps Mother is in prison, too. Perhaps the Communists will poison you with atheism. Perhaps, being brought up on the streets, you will become a delinquent. Maybe you will become a saint. But I have many saints around me. They are also sinners, and their only righteousness is that they have a part in the forgiveness of sins.

Mihai, you will need the only one who can forgive sins. Even non-Christians know the forgiveness of sins. They grant it to themselves after every deed which their own conscience considers ugly. But when I, a crook, grant myself, the crook, forgiveness for my crookedness, then I, the crook, am clever enough not to believe the absolution given to me, the crook, by me, the crook.

Only the Righteous One can absolve me from sin. You will sin, Mihai, whatever you become, whatever you believe. You will need a saviour, even if you become an atheist, because you will sometimes sin against your atheism. Nobody is a consistent atheist twenty-four hours a day. One atheist lecturer confessed to me how frightened he was when he had to speak against God in a former church building now turned into a club. Sadly, there is no atheist God. This man would have needed forgiveness for the sin of having wavered in his godless belief.

Mihai, you will need a saviour. Life will teach you that, in a greater or less measure, all men are liars. This will make you disbelieve any salvation brought by men. You need God as saviour. It is written that God has purchased the church with his own blood.[3] God became man, had blood, and shed it for our sins. Only this can save you.

He is a God, and therefore beyond our understanding. When you were small you could not understand why I would not let you throw a watch on the floor. It would have made such a nice noise. I showed you a poem by our greatest poet, Eminescu, and asked you what it was. You answered: "Black letters on white paper." That was all it was for you at that time. You did not know how to read.

So you cannot read the writing of God's providence. You will have to suffer, and you will not understand why. You may be even now picking food from a garbage heap, while in some rich countries the garbage vans carry away wasted food. You may be driven to despair. Perhaps you will one day sit in prison, too.

Because he is a God, his ways must be mysterious, as the doings of the scientist are mysterious to the illiterate. I have no idea why I have had to suffer so much.

But what I do know is that God is determined to make you and me into masterpieces. It took Goethe forty years to perfect *Faust*. Leonardo da Vinci worked for decades on the "Gioconda". I told you the story of the first, and I showed you the picture. Eminescu rewrote some thirty times his great poem "The Morning Star". God's hammer and chisel will hurt you again and again. The sculptor does not tell the marble what he intends to make out of it. When you have become a masterpiece of grace, admired by angels, you will understand the suffering.

Not understanding, only believing, cling to Jesus, the divine Saviour. The scars on his hands are the proof of his love towards you. The hand which strikes you bears the marks of wounds endured for you. Believe that your suffering is necessary for your own good and for the good of the whole of which you are only a small part.

And, bought by a sacrifice, lead a life of sacrifice. The sacrifice of Christ is not enough. St. Paul said: "I fill up on my part the penury of the afflictions of Christ."[4] What an amazing word – the penury of his afflictions. To be rejected by your own people, betrayed by your own disciple, deserted by nearly everyone, to be scourged, crowned with a crown of thorns, crucified and reviled – this is "a penury of afflictions"! What then would a richness of afflictions be? But St. Paul uses the same Greek word as is used in the Gospels about the widow who gave out of her penury. Many thousands of others have to sacrifice their liberty and lives to make the cross of the Lord known. Otherwise it is condemned to remain a poor thing unable to save mankind.

Choose, Mihai, the way of sacrifice. I cannot. I am deserting to another world. Do better than me, Mihai. Bear what I could not bear. Love Jesus and endure to the end.

Mihai, make Mother happy. Tell her that I loved her and that I am sorry I have sometimes been unkind to her.

Sermon to the Churches in the West

MY DEAR BROTHERS AND SISTERS IN THE WEST

The one who is speaking to you is a Christian isolated in a Communist prison cell.

For two years I have been speaking by spiritual telepathy to my former church congregation, and I believe it works.

Now I have decided to go one step further, and to speak to you who are in distant lands.

In order to succeed, I have kept silent for a long time. I have ceased to deliver sermons to my own people. I have ceased for a longer time even to speak to God. I did not allow any inner voice to disturb the quiet. I kept silence inwardly and outwardly. I remembered that, before the fall of Jericho, Joshua ordered the people: "Ye shall not shout, nor make any noise with your voice, neither shall any word proceed out of your mouth, until the day I bid you shout."[1] When the people shouted after such a prolonged silence, the wall fell down flat.[2] How far you can reach in the spirit depends on how long you have been silent.

The voice of Jesus reached the whole world and is still heard after two thousand years, because he imposed silence on himself until the age of thirty. Silence, although he had so much to say!

I have been silent for your sake. Now listen!

The man who has a narrow horizon cannot think rightly. A man who knows only what is happening in his own room may be killed the next moment by someone who has already penetrated into the next room with the intention of murdering him. If your horizon is your parish, your denomination or your country, you are doomed. What if another country has already prepared the weapons to kill you? What if some other religion has valuable insights unknown to you, which may prove that it can assure salvation?

Only the strategist who knows what is happening on the whole front can think correctly. "The world is my parish," said Wesley. The world (not in the sense of the earth, but of the cosmos), with all its inhabitants and its creator, is the horizon of the Christian. He does not stop at less than that.

Don't tell me that such a wide horizon is only for the highest church leaders, and not for rank-and-file Christians. There is no such thing as a rank-and-file Christian, because every Christian is of the highest rank. Every Christian is a partaker of the divine nature. God doesn't put anyone away in a file in the archives. There are no rank-and-file Christians. Christians think in terms of the whole cosmos and its creator, as they think in terms of infinity and eternity.

I, in my solitary cell, in the grip of the tuberculosis which has invaded my whole body, sit with the angels as in a theatre and watch everything that is happening, that has happened, and is yet to happen. I continue to be attached to my body only by a very weak fluidic tie. My spirit has escaped from the bedlam in which mankind with its accursed mentality is doomed to live.

Now I see reality as it is: a burden which I have to bear.

If God is in me, the whole responsibility of the cosmos becomes mine. "If a man love me, he will keep my words: and my Father will love him, and we will come unto him, and make our abode with him."[3] Don't tell me, Satan, that I have not kept his words. You don't know our human vocabulary. Jesus did not lay down as a condition for his abiding with us that we fulfil his word, but just that we keep it. I have not fulfilled it, but I have kept it unaltered. I have not accommodated Bible verses to my sins, but when I have committed sins I have left the word unaltered. Like David, I danced before the ark containing the tables of the commandments which I have broken in my personal life. But David did not abuse his royal powers to change the commandments.

So God abides in me. If he abides in me, he brings with him all his responsibilities. They become mine. That is why Jesus says that I have the power to remit sins or to retain them,[4] to bind and to loose.[5] If God lives in me and in you, it depends on us whether beauty will conquer, or whether mankind will deteriorate more and more.

If God the Father and Jesus Christ abide in a Christian, it becomes his task to change the perverted, the immoral, the obsessed, the ambitious, the robbers; to transform a neurotic world into a world full of serenity.

If the Father abides in me, every time anyone in the world says an "Our Father", he addresses the Godhead within me, too. I feel the prayers of all mankind addressed to me, as if my address – Cell number eleven in the prison of the Ministry of Interior Affairs in Bucharest – is in fact God's address.

I used to wonder why the Church repeats the Lord's prayer so often. Now I understand. Every time I say it, I am reminded that mankind expects me and my brethren, the bearers of God-head, to make his kingdom come – his kingdom of righteousness and joy. We have to see that his will is done on earth. We have to provide the hungry with the bread of life. We have to forgive.

Now I see the explanation of the words "Lead us not into temptation". God tempts nobody. But Godhead is in me. And I might tempt my fellow-man to sin. In saying these words, I am reminded of the many who wish to keep their innocence and pray to God that they may not be tempted. The prayer is addressed to me, too, because God is in me. I must not tempt.

It is I, and you, who must deliver the world from evil.

It was prophesied that God would gather the scattered Jews back into their former land. God did not do it from heaven. There was a man: Theodor Herzl. He created the Zionist movement, and this gave birth to the Jewish state, where Jews are now gathered from all countries. God brought it about through the Zionist leaders, and through the pioneers who brought their young lives as a sacrifice.

Men pray, "Deliver us from evil." Don't wait for a God in heaven to do this! Godhead is in you, as it is in me. The prayer is addressed to you, too. You must deliver mankind from the evil one. God's responsibilities are yours.

You, brothers and sisters in the West, are free. Don't you know about the evils of Communism? Some of you may be indifferent. But there is something worse than indifference. It is indifference to indifference. Some of you may not even care that the Church has become indifferent to the cries of millions of men martyred by the Communists.

When I say the prayer "Deliver us from evil", I don't address it to a God somewhere far away in heaven. I address it to you, those in whom God abides. All our prayers in these underground dungeons are an appeal to you, too. The Kabbala says: "God with Israel is God. God without Israel is not God." Even the greatest violinist can produce perfect music only if he has a good violin. What could he do without a good violin? What can God, to whom I pray, do if all his workers are on strike and his soldiers refuse to fight?

I see you congregated in your churches and praising God in beautiful songs. But why don't you leave God alone? According to the Talmud, God says: "O, that men would forget me and begin to love each other."

Don't you heed the word of Scripture? "To what purpose is the multitude of your sacrifices unto me?" saith the Lord: "I am full of burnt offerings . . . Bring no more vain oblations . . . Learn to do well . . . relieve the oppressed."[6] To relieve Christians oppressed by the Communists is a much more pleasing divine service than your holy masses and liturgies.

Abou Ben Adhem awoke one night from a dream – so runs the legend – and saw an angel writing in a golden book. He asked: "What writest thou?" The angel replied: "The names of those who love the Lord." He asked if his name was there, and the angel told him, "No." And so he begged:

"I pray thee, then,
Write me as one who loves his fellow men."
The angel wrote, and vanish'd. The next night
It came again with a great wakening light,
And show'd the names whom love of God had blest,
And lo! Ben Adhem's name led all the rest.[7]

Jesus said that the second commandment, to love your neighbour, is like the first, to love God. If you love us, the oppressed Christians in the Red camp, you love God, because God is within us, in cell eleven, and twelve, and thirteen, and in the cell with the rats and in the cell reserved for tortures.

I cannot tell you what to do for us. The pastors among us have been smitten, and the sheep are scattered. Care for these sheep, gather them in. Our Bibles have been confiscated. Our families eat garbage. I don't know how you can reach them. But you are the abode of the almighty and omniscient God. He must know. I speak to God. That means I speak to you. I say an "Our Father". Listen, it is addressed to you: "Our Father, which art in heaven." What heaven is more beautiful for him than your believing soul? He is in you. "Deliver us from evil." Communism is evil.

Brothers and sisters from the West, deliver us. *Amen.*

I Made Him Smile

JESUS

I wonder if Greek or Indian mythology is simply a collection of fantasies, or if it contains a dim apprehension of spiritual reality.

Has Agni, worshipped in India as the god of fire, any real existence? They call him god. I would rather call him angel. But I like him. And is it possible that you can exclude from heaven one being who pleases me, your beloved?

Queen Isabella of Spain said to Columbus: "I don't know if the land you go to seek exists. But if it does not exist, I am sure God will create it as a reward for your faith."

So, if Agni is only a mythological figure, you can make him exist, just in order to give me pleasure.

I like him because of the following story. It is said that, in the course of a severe persecution of his worshippers, one of them was burned at the stake. His soul came to heaven, but Agni refused to admit him. The believer protested: "But don't you know that I gave my life under torture for you?" "I know," replied Agni, "but while you were burning, you did not rejoice."

Don't you like this story? It reminds me of how you went to Gethsemane singing psalms.

I can imagine how sad you must be when a Christian who has died in prison comes to tell you how he has borne the cross for you, and has two witnesses to this fact: Brother Murmuring and Sister Disputing. You sang when you went to face your arrest.

Neither can I imagine your mother as *mater dolorosa*, the grieved mother weeping at the foot of the cross. She taught you from childhood that you were the Suffering Servant, that you would die by crucifixion, but would rise with the knowledge of having redeemed mankind. I see her going before you on the way to Calvary, singing to you psalms of encouragement, while the uninitiated daughters of Jerusalem wept.

She was a Jewess. On the very evening of your crucifixion the Passover ritual must have been performed in the house of St. John, during which the ritual prescribed singing. She must have sung on that day and, as she is holy, I believe that she did it whole-heartedly.

Before my arrest I saw certain mothers of young Christians who were in prison. Their faces shone for joy. They considered it a privilege to have martyrs for sons. The holy virgin must have been even more exalted.

So let us forget for a while, Jesus, that you and I are in prison. I am very sorry we are detained in a cell. Because it is your character to stay with your little brothers, if one of them is in a damp and dreary prison cell, you have to stay in prison, too. I may get a heavy sentence. You may have years of prison before you. You know it is not my fault. If you stand and knock at the door of a free man, it depends on him whether he opens the door or not. You knew that you would knock on my cell door in vain. The guards keep the key. So you came in through the locked door. Then you invited me to sup with you, which was good. But afterwards you wished to sup with me. I had not much to offer you. We have one slice of bread a week, and every day a bowl of dirty soup.

But let us forget all that, and do what prisoners all over the world do when they have company in their cell. They try to have a bit of fun.

I will begin by telling you a joke. You must have heard many jokes at the marriage feasts and in the houses of publicans, and you must have enjoyed at least some of them.

An elderly lady once accidentally sat on her false teeth and broke them. Her husband was in dismay. "What a catastrophe! What will you do now?" She answered: "Don't worry. Let us look on the bright side. It is better to sit on your false teeth than on your natural ones."

What optimism!

This reminds me to tell you the difference between an optimist and a pessimist. The optimist says: "Under this Communist régime we shall all become beggars." The pessimist replies: "But who shall we beg from?"

Come, Jesus, can't I make you laugh a little? True, the gospels speak of your weeping, and never about your laughter. But how is it, then, that children flocked round you? Children are not attracted to sad men.

I will tell you another story. This is sure to make you laugh.

A sultan once drove in a luxurious carriage over a bridge. The horses were frightened, overthrew the carriage, and the sultan fell into the river. On the bridge sat a beggar named Osman. He could not imagine the world without the sultan. So he jumped into the water and saved the sultan's life. Another carriage was brought, and the sultan invited the beggar to sit at his side, as an honour for saving his life.

While they were driving towards the palace, the sultan said: "Osman, I owe you my life. So I have decided to give you a sack full of gold coins. You will be happy and always remember me before Allah in your prayers. Are you satisfied with this reward?" The beggar was delighted, but the sultan regretted having promised so much. So he said: "It is not good for you to have so much money. You might be killed by robbers. I had better give you a hundred sheep. You will eat their meat and drink their milk and remember me before God. Are you satisfied with this?" The beggar, having no choice, agreed. But the sultan again regretted his generosity, and said: "There may be an epidemic, and your sheep will die. I had better give you a small hut. There you will live in peace and pray for me. Are you satisfied with this?" The beggar was happy to have at least a hut. But even this seemed too much for the sultan. By this time the carriage had entered the palace yard. The servants ran to meet it. The sultan said: "Give this man a good beating. Then he will surely remember me for his whole life."

You are weeping, Jesus. Isn't the story amusing?

I am sorry I have made you sad. Instead of laughing, you are crying. I should have thought of that. I have just remembered Dostoievsky's *Idiot*, the best portrait of a Christian character. He never laughed.

You are weeping because you see that my teeth have decayed through lack of sun and calcium. You thought of this, when I told you the joke about the false teeth. You are weeping because men rule over great countries, transforming other men into beggars, wiping out the rich instead of wiping out poverty. You did not enjoy the joke about optimism and pessimism. You weep because you yourself have been the victim of ingratitude. You were whipped like poor Osman because you saved lives. It was very tactless of me to tell you such a story.

How will you appear before the god Agni, Jesus? He will reproach you, too, for not being joyful. Just take it as another joke. I know the truth. Agni will appear before you, not the other way round. But the Indian religion is a very old one, older than the one you established. Old religions are very daring, and Agni might forget his position of utter inferiority before you. He might question you.

But until then, may I tell you something very frankly? You insist on sharing my cell. But it is not funny to be with you in here. Under the Nazis, I had many cell companions. Some of them made me forget all my sufferings. They knew how to make me laugh.

I have tried to make you laugh, but it is not possible. I wonder how it was in the furnace, in Daniel's day, when you were there with the three young men. You saved their bodies from being burned, just as my body miraculously survives the heavy attack of tuberculosis. Did you comfort their souls, or did you sadden them with your infinite sorrow? I think the latter must be the truth. Evidence of this is that, once released from the furnace, they remained for ever silent. Not one word more was heard from them, not even a word of heroism.

I sometimes have the feeling that you come to us who suffer, not in order to comfort us, but to draw comfort from us. You called the Holy Spirit "the Comforter". Why, then, did the

Comforter have to descend on you at your baptism? Were you – are you – in great need of comfort?

Most of the great mystics have experienced the dark night of the soul, when they felt terribly alone, without you. St. Gertrude prayed: "You are I and I am you." If this is true of mystics, then the dark night through which they passed was only a mirror of the dark night in your own soul. You, who have been tempted like us in all things, must have known spiritual dryness, too. The words of the Song of Solomon must have had meaning for you too: "By night on my bed I sought him whom my soul loveth: I sought him, but I found him not. I will rise now, and go about the city in the streets and in the broad ways I will seek him whom my soul loveth: I sought him, but I found him not."[1] You know what it means to be without any comfort.

How stupid of me to try to tell you jokes. Your depression is too deep. You cannot laugh.

When you were about four or five you were told about the children who died in Bethlehem, and about Rachel weeping for them. It was the man who received you into the stable who was to blame. If he had not given you shelter their innocent blood would not have been shed. As a grown man you brought the wrath of God upon Israel by demanding love from those who have no love, by demanding that wolves should be lambs, and by provoking your own crucifixion, which was inevitable after such demands.

And so there followed the punishment of God.

Since then, all who receive and love you have to bear a heavy cross. They have to crucify their lusts – a painful task. The pain may be as great as that which you endured on Golgotha. Some have to die in prison. Some are tortured. Some are killed.

And you suffer the sufferings of them all. You still endure far greater pain than we, because we feel only our own sufferings. You feel the sufferings of all. You need comfort more than we do.

Jokes were the wrong way to comfort you. I apologise. I am

only human. I meant well. I wanted to make you happy. I remember how St. Onofrei as a child offered to your image half of his apple, and you stretched out a hand from the image to take it. I remember the Orthodox tradition about the circus boy who did his juggling act in front of your icon, and how, when the monks tried to stop him, you smiled in the icon, showing your approval. But that was in the early centuries when Christians were children and could believe such things. You must have been happier. Now we have systematic theology in which St. Onofrei has no place.

Now you need a different kind of comfort.

The only comfort I can give you is to tell you that I, and thousands of others who suffer, love you. Even if the beast rules the world, when our candles burn out our last words will be, "Beloved Jesus."

Don't be depressed by our suffering. Believe me, we can bear it. We can bear it more easily if we know that you are happy in your heaven and enjoying the fellowship of the angels and the glorified saints. We love you, Jesus. Be happy.

Look, I will do something like the boy in the circus. Our prison is an old one. The bourgeois régime built it for the Communists. Now the Communists are using it for their own enemies. Chalk is crumbling from the walls. I will take a piece of chalk and draw your picture on the door. Here are the curls, the beard, the eyes, the nose. And now it depends on me. If I give an upward curve to your lips, you will have a smiling face. You will not be able to help it. So I will do it. And now you are smiling again, as you did for St. Onofrei, or when you had a St. Rose of Lima, to whom you could say, "Rose of my heart."

I have made you smile. Hallelujah!

Now, just be happy for a while. And please don't reproach me for breaking the second commandment by making an image. To make you, the Man of Sorrows, smile, is more important than the entire decalogue.

Who can live without an image? The mystics claim unmediated communion with God, but when you compare them with each other you can see that even they had fellowship with God, not as he is, but with an image of him formed by their individual background. Even yogis, when they arrive at perfect imagelessness, have an image of imagelessness given to them by Hindu tradition. In other circumstances these same men would have had a different mystical experience. We all draw pictures of you in our minds. I have drawn one on the door to make you smile.

And you, reason, be silent. Don't tell me that it was only the picture of Jesus which smiled, and not Jesus himself. He is himself an image – "the express image of God's person".[2] If you challenge my right to attribute to Jesus the smile in my picture, then you have to challenge the fact that whoever sees him, the image of the Father, sees the Father himself.

This is a day of great triumph for me. I have made you, Jesus, smile. I pray that I may do it always. *Amen.*

Clean Every Whit

DEAR BROTHERS AND SISTERS

When they take us out of our cells to lead us away for interrogation, they always blindfold us. We must not get to know the layout of the prison. It might help us to escape. I don't mind. They blindfolded him, too.[1] And whenever they do it to us, they do it to him again.

I remember how St. Paulinus wrote that Christ did not die only once but was the Lamb slain from the beginning of the world. He was murdered in Abel, offered up in Isaac, persecuted in Jacob, betrayed in Joseph, blinded in Samson, sawn asunder in Isaiah. I have often pondered the thought with which he goes on, that Christ's passion continued after his resurrection. It was he who was stoned in St. Stephen, flayed in the person of St. Bartholomew. He was roasted upon St. Lawrence's gridiron, burned in St. Polycarp, frozen in the lake where stood the forty martyrs of Cappadocia.

St. Hilary goes even further, saying that the sacrament of Christ's death is to be accomplished only by suffering all the sorrows of humanity.

It is he who is blindfolded by my jailers.

Everything transitory is only a parable, says Goethe. So this blindfolding must have a spiritual meaning too. Why do the Communists blindfold not only their fellow-men but also the divine Christ? Why did his judges blindfold him two thousand years ago?

If I had to defend them before God, I would tell him: "Understand them, and forgive them. They are simply retaliating. You blindfolded them first. Is it not written that you have 'blinded their eyes, and hardened their hearts; that they should not see with their eyes, nor understand with their hearts, and be converted'?[2] You were the first to blindfold men. You cannot condemn them for doing the same to you. I have had to pass through unspeakably bitter experiences. I had to be spat on and mocked and beaten before I understood why you did it. They, lacking the experience, could not know why."

It is a terrible thing to have one's spiritual eyes opened. It is a blessing from God to have them blinded and not be converted by the devious and difficult path of understanding. St. John, the seer, when he saw Jesus in his divine glory, fell at his feet as if dead.[3] Which of us could bear to see all the seven heads and ten horns of the red dragon of Communism?[4] Who could understand why this beast has seven crowns on his head, when Jesus had only a crown of thorns? What a good thing God has blinded our eyes and hardened our understanding, so that we should not be converted by seeing or understanding but simply by loving and trusting. It is only right that there should be nobody more blind than he that is perfect, the Lord's servant.[5]

The enemies of Jesus two thousand years ago did not understand, and neither do the Communists today, that nobody can see God and live; that those whom God loves most and wishes to be his servants must be blind to the final realities. The Communists retaliate by hating God. That is why they blindfold us and beat us while we are blindfolded, an excessive torture because you don't know from which side the blow will come, and you cannot defend yourself at least by bending your head the other way.

I can understand our torturers, because I also had a grudge against God for not answering my questions and not showing me if there was any hope. But today I have decided to accept blindness.

I was washed long ago in the blood of Christ. But today I have told him I will give him my feet to be washed, too; my feet which, walking through the valley of deep sorrow, have become soiled with the dust of murmuring against God. Then I shall be clean every whit.[6]

I read, when I was free, that the Red Indians, wondering at the paleness of the white men's skins, removed their shoes to see if their feet were white, too. My feet must be white. When my torturers beat me on the soles of my feet they have the right to see clean feet, whiter than snow. Jesus said: "He that is washed needeth not save to wash his feet, but is clean every whit." My feet may be swollen because of prolonged hunger and the other experiences through which I have passed, but those who beat me have the right to see the beautiful feet of a bride of Christ who brings, even to them, good tidings.[7] I must have my feet washed by Jesus. He is far away. But I preach in his name, by morse code. I have given sacraments in his name. Why should I not wash my feet in his name, believing that he himself is doing it?

Down with you, rags. I have no shoes. For two years I have walked in them, to and fro across my cell, three steps one way, three steps the other, chanting prayers in the Jewish manner. For two years I have danced in them. They have done their job. A shoemaker gave them to me as a present before I went to prison and told me: "Use them in the service of the Lord." He did not know, neither did I, that they would be used to dance in the Lord's honour.

On one foot I have only rags. On the other I have a fine woman's stocking. I found it in the toilet. How and why a female prisoner left it behind there, I don't know. I needed it badly. I took it. We don't think in terms of property here.

I have undressed my feet. The cement is cold. The water which I pour over them is icy. What was the water like which Jesus used to wash the disciples' feet? Perhaps it was very cold, too. On that same night, the guards had to kindle a fire in the temple yard to warm themselves. Perhaps St. Peter shrank back from the coldness of the water when he said: "Thou shalt not wash my feet." What Jesus did on that evening happened on the icy peaks of the highest spirituality, where God takes the humblest form of a servant. It is not easy to have your feet washed in the almost freezing water from those divine springs.

I wash my feet in the name of Jesus. It is he who washes my feet. Listen, God; listen, angels and demons; listen, brethren and Communist torturers. I have washed my feet. Now I am clean every whit. Listen, you victims of my past life.

I don't know what my future will be. Perhaps I shall break down under torture and become a traitor. Perhaps I shall lose my faith. Perhaps I shall earn the martyr's crown. Perhaps I shall be released only to commit great sins. Perhaps prison life will have destroyed my character. Perhaps I shall do great deeds for God. I tremble to think about Hans Nielson Hauge, the great Norwegian evangelist, who was imprisoned for his faith some two centuries ago. He, who had set Norway aflame with love for Christ, lost his simple faith in prison. Who knows what fate is reserved by Providence for me?

But I need not worry. Jesus has washed my feet. Jesus is in me. He is my real me. I am his real he. I speak and act in his name. It was not I myself but he who washed my feet, and I will believe that now I am and shall remain clean every whit.

Once, having passed through a terrible torture, I tapped through to a pastor near me: "What can I do? I have lost my faith." He tapped back: "But did you ever believe?" I replied: "Certainly I did." His answer was: "It is written, 'Blessed is she that believed.'[8] The verb is in the past tense. To have believed is enough. Rely on this."

I am clean every whit, and I shall remain so because I have once been so. Betrayals and gross sins may come. They will never change my status before God. I recall that Spurgeon once said that the past, present and future sins of believers are all forgiven. I cannot remember on which Bible text he based this teaching. But if it is false, that is his business with God. God should not have given him such a great name among his children if he taught falsely. I will rely on his word.

I am, and remain, clean every whit through the humility of Jesus Christ, who washed my feet.

My torturers, I offer you a precious gift. I offer to your rubber truncheons the soles of feet washed by Jesus himself, feet which, like those of the angels, have to be covered [9] because they are surrounded by a divine halo. You will beat my feet, and the halo around them will speak to you of the holiness of the one who humbled himself for me. *Amen.*

Epilogue

It was not my intention to give you another exposition of Christian truth. For this you have your Bible, your church and your religious teacher, who answers for your soul before God.

I know your problems. Religious teachers of Christianity differ widely in the most essential questions. There are so many divisions, and in each, especially in Protestantism, innumerable subdivisions. You may understand that I had thoughts apart under conditions apart. But you would like to know what my theology and moral rules are now, when my outward life has returned to normal.

I have no original ideas to offer. I am not an original religious thinker. I believe that theology is like wine: the older the better. If you were to ask what I think about one or other religious matter, my answer would in general be that of any average Evangelical pastor, with one of the slight variations which are the beauty and privilege of Protestantism, and the result of the liberty which it has brought. But I could never define, finally and absolutely, what my theology is, and I will tell you why.

I once tried to explain "systematic theology" to a Russian pastor of the Underground church, who had never seen a whole New Testament. Systematically, I began to explain to him the teaching about the Godhead, about its unity in three persons, the teaching about original sin, about the fall, about salvation, about the church, about the sacraments, about the Bible as infallible revelation. He listened attentively. When I had finished, he put to me a most surprising question: "Have those who thought out these theological systems and wrote them down in such perfect order ever carried a cross?" He went on: "A man cannot think systematically even when he has a bad toothache. How can a man who is carrying a cross think systematically? But a Christian has to be more than the bearer of a heavy cross; he shares Christ's crucifixion. The pains of Christ are his, and the pains of all creation. There is no grief and no suffering in the whole world which should not grieve him also. If a man is crucified with Christ, how can he think systematically? Can there be that kind of thought on a cross? Jesus himself thought unsystematically on the cross. He began with forgiveness; he dreamed of a paradise in which even a robber had a place; then he despaired that perhaps there might be no place in paradise even for him, the Son of God. He felt himself forsaken. Then all at once he remembered his mother. But the thirst was so unbearable that he forgot about her and asked for water. Then he surrendered his spirit into his Father's hand. But there followed no serenity, only a loud cry. Thank you for what you have been trying to teach me. I have the impression that you were only repeating, without much conviction, what others have taught you. Systematic theology of any kind is impossible in Christianity."

This pastor, uncultured theologically, did not even know that he was thinking the same way as Kierkegaard, the most eminent Lutheran theologian who, from another standpoint, also denied that a Christian can ever speak academically about Christ. A Christian is a person who is madly in love with Christ. Juliet could not make a peroration about the anatomy of Romeo's body. She could only caress him and express to everybody her burning desire for him.

I think the same way as that Underground pastor. So I could only put in writing some of the thoughts I had when I was in solitary confinement. By now many of these thoughts have changed. That is the fate of thoughts. The thoughts of today will not last either. They may change again tomorrow, if the Communists kidnap me and put me in a solitary cell again. Thoughts about the Godhead, just like thoughts about any other subject, belong to the transient world. In our solitary cells, we lived in the sphere of eternity.

I felt it to be my duty to lead you by a roundabout way into this sphere and not to bother you with the thoughts which I hold today. Thoughts are a reflection in our mind, true or distorted, of reality. We should try to apprehend the reality of God and not remain in the sphere of words and thoughts. Thoughts about God are not God. Only God is God. Never be satisfied with anything else than God himself. I am in fellowship with all men who seek God – to seek him means to have found him, says St. Augustine – and with all those who bear the marks of suffering. A Christian, even if he is a healthy young millionaire, is a man of sorrows. That is what makes him a Christian: that he apppropriates to himself the sufferings of Christ and of all creation.

As regards moral problems, ask the pastor of your church. Morals are concerned with the relationship between man and man in the sight of God. I am still living basically in solitary confinement. There the relationship is only with God. Morals cease to exist. But looking out from there to the church and the world, where man enters into contact with man, I can tell you two things.

First, there is a tremendous value in the traditional Biblical standard of morality. If it did not have the whole weight of the Godhead and of thousands of years of man's experience behind it, how is it that every sin committed even thirty years ago gave such painful remorse in prison? By sinning today, you prepare for yourself hours of regret in the future.

Secondly, understand that nobody can live an endless crucifixion. Jesus was on the cross only a few hours. When a man experiences great suffering, or the pain of an unsatisfied imperious longing, condemn him if he yields after a few hours. But after years of struggling a man may fall under the burden of the cross. To understand, to love and to free him from this cross is also a part of morality. Love is the interpretation which God himself gives to all Bible verses and commandments. I know nothing better than St. Augustine's words: "Love God, and do what you will."

"Of making many books there is no end."[1] There are enough

188

books of Christian doctrine and morality. I did not feel called
to add another one.

I wanted to describe to you the hell of Communist solitary
confinement. I wanted to illustrate for you the words of the
Creed that "he descended into hell", to suffer himself its
anguish, and to take upon himself its terrors as he has taken
the sins of mankind, and to bring even there a ray of the light
of God.

Every man must be believed in his own art. When it comes
to the things of the spiritual life, you must believe those who
know it thoroughly. St. Catherine of Genoa said about hell:
"When we shall have departed from this life in a state of sin,
God will withdraw from us his goodness and will leave us to
ourselves, and yet not altogether, since he wills that in every
place his goodness shall be found and not his justice alone.
And if a creature could be found that did not, in some degree,
participate in the divine goodness, that creature would be, one
might say, as malignant as God is good", which would deny the
sole absoluteness of God.

Communist solitary confinement with the remembrance of
past sins is a corner of hell. There were times when I looked at
the cup of water which I had in my cell to convince myself that
I was not yet in hell. I knew that in hell there was no water.

But even in the moments of utter doubt and utter despair,
we were not left to ourselves entirely. The one who promised
"I am with you always"[2] (in Hebrew he could say only *bekol
iom*, which means literally translated "every day the whole
day") has proved to be faithful. So we were able to overcome.

There are thousands of other Christians in solitary confinement today, in Red China, North Korea, Vietnam, Russia,
Albania, Rumania, Czechoslovakia and so on. Will you stand
by them? Will you send your winged guardian angel to tell them
that you love them? Will you consider as your responsibility the
work of the Underground church, from which they have been
snatched away, that it may continue to grow in their absence?

To make this appeal to you was my purpose in publishing this
book.

References

Preface
[1] Hebrews 13. 3
[2] Psalm 45. 10
[3] Psalm 45. 11
[4] Song of Solomon 1. 5

God's Unjust Laws
[1] Genesis 2. 18
[2] Isaiah 1. 18
[3] Matthew 5. 45
[4] Ezekiel 20. 25
[5] John 14. 1
[6] Song of Solomon 3. 11
[7] Revelation 8. 1–4
[8] Psalm 40. 6
[9] Numbers 35
[10] Song of Solomon 5. 8
[11] Matthew 11. 12
[12] Mark 5

A Christian Encounters the Angel Gabriel
[1] Micah 1. 11–15; 5. 2
[2] Acts 4. 27–28
[3] Isaiah 1. 18; Psalm 51. 7

The Mother of the Lord
[1] Revelation 4. 2–3
[2] Revelation 12. 1
[3] Genesis 1. 27
[4] John 19. 25
[5] Matthew 12. 50

Duty Never Ends
[1] Revelation 2. 16
[2] Matthew 6. 22

Samson in Prison
[1] 1 Timothy 1. 15
[2] Luke 13. 1
[3] Judges 4. 21
[4] 2 Chronicles 18. 19–20
[5] Judges 5. 24
[6] Psalm 96

Sermon to My Own Soul
 [1] Matthew 4. 4   [2] Matthew 23. 17, 23
 [3] 1 Corinthians 10. 22   [4] 2 Thessalonians 1. 5

Word Made Flesh
 [1] Psalm 134. 1   [2] Ephesians 2. 10
 [3] Ephesians 3. 11–12

Gagged Again
 [1] Genesis 1. 31   [2] James 1. 19

Visible Wounds
 [1] Mark 9. 43–47   [2] 1 Thessalonians 3. 3
 [3] Luke 16. 26   [4] Revelation 12. 3

Binzea
 [1] Genesis 1. 27   [2] John 10. 11–12
 [3] Genesis 19. 17   [4] 1 John 1. 7
 [5] Luke 24. 39   [6] 1 Corinthians 12. 12
 [7] Colossians 1. 24   [8] Matthew 5. 13

Sermon to the Victims of My Life
 [1] *Acts of John* 94–96. *The Apocryphal New Testament* trs.
 Montague Rhodes James, quoted by permission of the
 Clarendon Press, Oxford
 [2] Romans 6. 23   [3] Matthew 5. 21
 [4] Matthew 5. 28   [5] Acts 24. 14
 [6] 2 Corinthians 3. 3

Ani-hu
 [1] Matthew 25. 31–40   [2] Acts 9. 4
 [3] John 14. 9   [4] Matthew 17. 4

Sick of Love
 [1] Matthew 8. 16–17   [2] 1 Corinthians 3. 10
 [3] Psalm 18. 26   [4] Exodus 3. 14

The Fullest Sabbath
 [1] John 4. 23   [2] Acts 23. 3–6

There Is No God
[1] Psalm 14. 1   [2] Job 6. 2–3

The Unreasonableness of Love
[1] John 9. 41   [2] 1 Corinthians 1. 25
[3] Psalm 104. 21   [4] Philippians 4. 15

The Lesson of the Cell with the Rats
[1] Luke 18. 14   [2] Acts 17. 28
[3] Mark 15. 34 RV margin   [4] Song of Solomon 1. 16
[5] John 2. 10

Talk With My Son Mihai
[1] Matthew 21. 16   [2] John 10. 18, 11
[3] Acts 20. 28   [4] Colossians 1. 24

Sermon to the Churches in the West
[1] Joshua 6. 10   [2] Joshua 6. 20
[3] John 14. 23   [4] John 20. 23
[5] Matthew 16. 19   [6] Isaiah 1. 11–17
[7] Leigh Hunt, *Abou Ben Adhem*

I Made Him Smile
[1] Song of Solomon 3. 1–2   [2] Hebrews 1. 3

Clean Every Whit
[1] Luke 22. 64   [2] John 12. 40
[3] Revelation 1. 17   [4] Revelation 12. 3
[5] Isaiah 42. 19   [6] John 13. 10
[7] Isaiah 52. 7   [8] Luke 1. 45
[9] Isaiah 6. 2

Epilogue
[1] Ecclesiastes 12. 12   [2] Matthew 28. 20